AFRICAN POLITICAL, ECONOMIC AND SECURITY ISSUES

KNOWLEDGE TO ACTION BY RAPPROCHEMENT

COUNSEL TO ACTORS SEEKING IMPACT THROUGH POLICY AND REFORM OF INSTITUTIONS IN CENTRAL AFRICA

African Political, Economic and Security Issues

Additional books in this series can be found on Nova's website under the Series tab.

Additional e-books in this series can be found on Nova's website under the e-book tab.

AFRICAN POLITICAL, ECONOMIC AND SECURITY ISSUES

KNOWLEDGE TO ACTION BY RAPPROCHEMENT

COUNSEL TO ACTORS SEEKING IMPACT THROUGH POLICY AND REFORM OF INSTITUTIONS IN CENTRAL AFRICA

PETER N. MBILE

NOVINKA

New York

Library of Congress Cataloging-in-Publication Data

Mbile, Peter N.

Knowledge to action by rapprochement : counsel to actors seeking impact through policy and reform of institutions in Central Africa / editors: Peter N. Mbile (World Resources Institute, Yaounde, Cameroon, and Washington DC, USA).

pages cm

Includes bibliographical references and index.

ISBN-13: 978-1-62618-355-1 (soft cover)

ISBN-10: 1-62618-355-4 (soft cover)

1. Africa, Central--Politics and government--1960- 2. Natural resources--Africa, Central--Management. 3. Africa, Central--Economic conditions--1960- 4. Natural resources--Africa, Central--Management--Citizen participation. I. Title.

JQ2720.A58M395 2013

333.750967--dc23

2013014125

Published by Nova Science Publishers, Inc. † New York

CONTENTS

Preface		**vii**
Executive Summary		**ix**
Chapter 1	Central Africa Context: Resource Governance and Wellbeing	**1**
Chapter 2	Knowledge to Action through Policy in Central Africa	**17**
List of Terms		**45**
References		**55**
Index		**57**

PREFACE

This book provides counsel to actors seeking impact through policy and reform of institutions in countries of Central Africa. The content is based largely on the author's own intuitions drawn from more than 22 years of working experience in Central Africa.

For illustrative purposes the intuitions draw lessons from selected examples of policy processes in Cameroon and the Democratic Republic of Congo, where the author has on-the-ground experience. The book also legitimately draws from more economically advanced societies, notably Europe and North America from which the author has working and educational experience and therefore, believes important lessons can be learned.

DISCLAIMER

These intuitions, points of view and arguments should be judged on their own merit, in relation to general human development in the Central African context. They may not be considered a reflection of the official positions of the author's employers, nor those of the author's associates, or any others whose work and perspectives may benefit from its content.

EXECUTIVE SUMMARY

This book is about a proposition for *Rapprochement.* It focuses on the forest resources sector in countries of Central Africa, although it remains applicable to other natural resources management domains. It articulates arguments around a framework to vigorously bring actors together in real-time – or forge a *Rapprochement*; develop useful policies and grow effective institutions for rapid social and economic development. It is conceived to be applicable to individual national and sub national contexts.

The arguments and propositions are developed against a background of continuing unease that most natural resource policy frameworks for Central African countries are either not producing significant social and economic benefits for ordinary citizens, or are not doing so quickly enough to roll back poverty. Some explanations are put forward to help clarify perceived separation of actors and sluggishness in transformative decision-making using knowledge to action pathways through policy and allied mechanisms in the region. As backdrop and rational for a framework of *Rapprochement* – or bringing actors together in real-time, important constraints to evolving useful policies and effective institutions articulated in this book are summarized below:

i. Current forestry and other natural resources law enforcement and governance processes in Central Africa suggest a predominance of the absolute supremacy of often top-down, regular State law. Much less emphases are placed on democratic governance; fully participatory, time-bound reflections, planning and actions as can be facilitated by a process where actors systematically work together – in a vigorous framework of *Rapprochement*. In these young Central African States which are hemorrhaging young talent through out-migration, it is critical that social and economic development, law enforcement and governance, be characterized not just by regulatory aspects of unfamiliar policies, but by processes which inspire trust and confidence by addressing shared needs. Good policies should directly address livelihoods of ordinary folks, not just instruct them on the dos and don'ts, while catering largely to the needs of more well-to-do and influential interests.

ii. There is useful evidence from North America, Europe and East Asia that, well-funded and country-specific visions of policy change and reform of institutions have been important drivers of human social development and economic transformation. In Central Africa on the other hand, major processes of policy change and reform of institutions remain weakly relevant to economic and social development of many ordinary citizens. Instead, numerous policy mechanisms are in place to help enhance performance of global companies, international business initiatives and marketing mechanisms, without evidence of significant local buy-in of these processes from grassroots and ordinary citizens. As a consequence, impacts of some national policies and institutions appear to be relevant often only in name to the priorities of grassroots groups and ordinary citizens in Central Africa. In some extreme cases, existing policies and institutions even perceive grassroots communities (at the core of which are indigenous groups, rural people, women, the unemployed, other vulnerable groups or their representatives) not as the raison d'être for policy, but as problems to be addressed through the policy!

iii. Many knowledge centers or independent analysts, carry-out research on policy and institutions in Central Africa using rigid protocols, analyses and peer-review processes often strongly influenced by thinking and models from advanced policy contexts of Europe and North America. Many of these are only weakly tailored to local contexts. Especially, many of such analysis protocols appear to be only weakly adapted to the rapidly evolving, multi-actor and multi-sector decision-making prerogatives in Central Africa. Although efforts are often made to adapt analytical tools to local contexts, these have remained insufficient in some important areas. For instance, the tools are not often clear about how historical and geo-political factors which are critical determinants of behavior in Central Africa are to be handled. For such reasons, some emergent recommendations and format of policy dialogues often tend to be only conceptually relevant to protection of low-income citizens – although such protection clauses are often prominent in State Constitutions. Numerous post-independence policy changes and institutional reform actions have thus seemed somewhat disconnected from the everyday aspirations of ordinary citizens in the region.

iv. In a consolidating context of poverty and environmental change, these methodological and philosophical constraints in policy and institutions analyses both conspire to justify a need to radically reinvent policy and institutions analyses procedures by addressing some specific mindsets and constraints: some of these are outlined below;

- The assumption that those charged with making public policy decisions in Central Africa are just waiting to adopt and use published recommendations coming out of policy analyses is not accurate.
- The nature of the intermediate and final products of numerous scientific, policy analyses processes; comprising articles, briefs and other printed materials are often in formats that are only weakly consumed, therefore insufficiently applied, if at all, in the Central Africa region.
- The manner of policy and institutions analyses processes tend to comprise of project-based activities often executed within [short] fixed time-fames. This does not often match with the diffuse, multi-level, multi-actor, nature of the problems, needs of clients, socio-economic peculiarities, or even timing of opportunities, given the evolving complexity in Central Africa.
- Faced with reputational risks, and fearful of engaging too closely with the evolving problem context of Central Africa, some organizations performing these analyses prefer to protect themselves in the comfort zones of their institutional excellence goals; by completely avoiding engagement and preferring to work only indirectly in the region.

v. Forms of interaction and or separation between knowledge centers and change agents on the one hand, and those charged with making public policy decisions on the other, holds back uptake of knowledge by the latter group in the development process. This separation creates accumulation of knowledge in the knowledge centers, creating possibility for self-gratification, complacency, even smugness, while denying appropriate technology developers, development agents and those charged with making public policy decisions, the timeliness, information and tools they need to bring about change. This perceived isolation by knowledge centers can further heighten their fears of reputational risks, while users of knowledge are left to their own devices to take actions and make public policy decisions without the benefits of the latest technology, information or tools.

vi. As State administrations in Central Africa are left to their own devices when knowledge centers become uneasy about engaging too closely, these State entities can consolidate around their prerogatives – some more than others. In that consolidation [often driven by need for cash to address domestic budgets and pressures for greater democratic governance], they then become vulnerable to propositions from powerful multinationals or private equity firms [offering immediate solution to urgent problems], and who seek, not direct local development goals, but equity in global markets for commodities; and profits for their shareholders, but requiring natural resources access rights from local governments. When knowledge centers shy away from engagements that can moderate the actions of aggressive foreign investments, multinational firms can exert too much influence, sometimes leading to unfortunate, irreversible consequences for vulnerable groups and sustainable environmental management. The results are investments whose benefits neither trickle down, nor build capacity locally for a vibrant market economy; but instead, can create social problems and economic despair amongst ordinary folks.

So, when knowledge centers and other change agents become separated from those charged with making public policy decisions in decision-making centers, the main losers are those who otherwise would benefit from progressive policy change and institutional reform – often, vulnerable grassroots populations.

Structural separation between the powerful and/or procedures considered legal on the one hand; from the vulnerable and/or actions considered legitimate on the other, is a major factor constraining transition from knowledge to action through policy and institutions in Central Africa. *Rapprochement*, interpreted here as 'bringing *actors,* not just *stakeholders,* together', is thus proposed as a simple, yet robust and organic long-term solution which can finally unite the legal with the legitimate; the powerful with the vulnerable at multiple levels, literally forcing them to seek common solutions through planning, analyses, production activities and social change.

Therefore, the process of *Rapprochement* for policy change and reform of institutions in Central Africa, to be applied at national and sub national levels will comprise of five main components;

1. A relevant vision which articulates what success would look like within the specific policy and institutional change context; this can be relevant to a region, a province or a territory [as applicable to the specific country] where the specific outcomes [or behavior change] will be expected
2. A theoretical framework which facilitates development of hypotheses, thereby enhancing comparisons of a local agenda for *Rapprochement* with similar notions [from theory and practice elsewhere], and making adaptation and replication possible. This should make the principle comparable within and across country contexts.
3. A country/region-specific, real-world, '*bread and butter'* or livelihoods example or model. *Rapprochement* as a framework for analyzing policies and institutions is about social and economic development of ordinary citizens. Implementation for each country/region must therefore be built around a national level [or one from a similar context], evolving success story to be emulated, adapted; and against which progress can be monitored and evaluated. This aspect of *Rapprochement* should unite (i) the vision and (ii) the conceptual framework and (iii) facilitate data collection and analyses.
4. The *modus operandi* for *Rapprochement:* describing the 'nuts and bolts' or the mechanics of the '*bread and butter'* innovation; what new institutions need to be created or existing ones modified/strengthened? What their terms of references should be? And how they should function in alignment with existing National Annual Work Plans of major, relevant institutions? Which existing levels and relevant natural resources sector of Government should be given priority in *Rapprochement* in order to have the greatest impact; reach the most people, most cost-effectively, within the shortest possible time frame?
5. Final steps will comprise, description of the process of policy development; recording and deliberation of rules of procedure [identification of policy options] and pre-requisites for success, [and recommendations/adaptations] to be announced/published

beforehand; their adoption and or codification as needed. The timeframes within which these would be tried; nature of data collection and analyses to evaluate successes due to application of the guidelines; the definition of indicators of success, based on the vision for the policy; the rules and procedures for evaluation; responsibilities, modalities and timeframe for revision and review.

Chapter 1

CENTRAL AFRICA CONTEXT: RESOURCE GOVERNANCE AND WELLBEING

INTRODUCTION AND DEFINITION OF *RAPPROCHEMENT*

In a context of climate change, positive correlation will exist between activities that enhance wellbeing of ordinary citizens and the ability of communities to adapt to nefarious environmental changes (WRI Straw Objectivc on Adaptation, 2010). This statement is also true for Central Africa.

Unfortunately, poverty remains widespread in Central African countries where ownership rights of the majority of ordinary citizens to productive resources; land, forests and other natural resources remains very weak. The currently weak, formal ownership situation persists largely because State institutions are the dominant legal owners of most high-value natural resources in the region.

For instance in a constitutional democracy like the United States of America, greater than 65% of forests and woodlands are privately owned. So, despite post-independence constitutional guarantees of citizen's rights in Central African countries, comparative control of resources by State authorities of centralized and decentralized services, and by ordinary citizens in rural areas, remain in favor of the State. As a consequence, existing policy instruments linking ordinary rural citizens and low-income urban ones in particular, to institutions at higher levels of decision-making are not perceived as promoting co-ownership of productive resources and participation.

To-date, complicated notions of how to strengthen these linkages have not only fallen short, but have in some cases, created new challenges which have only served to eclipse original resource equity problems, without providing new solutions.

Linkages or lack thereof, between lower level communities in need, and higher level decision making institutions, have less to do with physical or geographic proximity. Instead, divergences exist between the needs and preferences of ordinary citizens and the core priorities of those charged with making public policy decisions in State institutions.

Following independence from colonial countries, significant differences have evolved and become entrenched between priorities of resident communities and of public decision-making authorities. This separation is resulting to isolation of the parties from each other, and has made the occurrence of poverty, more apparent in distant, rural communities or within low-income urban ones. The separation has dampened individual initiative across countries, weakened innovation in indigenous private sectors, increasing business risk and weakened overall economic activity.

Furthermore, divergences in priorities between institutions of State and of ordinary citizens have enhanced the proliferation of new entities and duplicitous functions, encouraging resource wastage. Separation between the government and the governed has also served to shield ordinary citizens from progressive national institutions or even from external collaborators sharing the aspirations and committed to work towards providing solutions to citizens' problems.

Such progressive national and international partners remain nevertheless, convinced [for lack of other viable mechanisms] that the most effective way to reach ordinary citizens is via existing public institutions. It is therefore urgent to conceive incentives and mechanisms to enable these parties to work together effectively.

By growing policies and institutions from within, to provide incentives for ordinary citizens and State authorities to work together, a *Rapprochement* can be created and sustained beyond the project phase.

One way to grow useful policies and effective institutions from within, and gradually minimize separation between priorities of ordinary citizens and core business of Government departments, is by cultivating a new work ethic of 'coming together' or of *Rapprochement*: between actors at multiple sectors of activity and at multiple levels of decision making. For such *Rapprochement* to then engender the desired transformation, it should be mediated by meaningful '*bread and butter*' activities and results (low hanging fruits) which change behavior and lives in the process.

Such *Rapprochement* should operate at all desired levels and sectors, implemented by affected actors who must demonstrate that they are learning from the process and therefore, willing to evaluate the usefulness of the knowledge gained, based on the results achieved.

Rapprochement between ordinary citizens and decision-making authorities can represent a break from both the post-colonial legacy of separation and that of 'projects', to constitute a substantial re-think of how to grow good policies and useful institutions in today's complexity of globalization and democratization. Not so that these policies and institutions then produce desired results by themselves, but so that, they sustain and strengthen positive interactions, and impacts, legitimizing and focusing on early impacts and immediate priorities of the actors. *Rapprochement* can then become the essential mechanism for linking policies and institutions, to action and development.

To fully appreciate the need for such a re-think, a substantial emersion in resource governance in terms of theories, the status quo and current context in Central Africa, vis-à-vis some global examples is needed. As foreword to resource governance, a possible context of *Rapprochement* must be built on a sound foundation of resource governance mediating the relationship between parties working together in real-time. Such a foundation is only possible if a context of rule of law exists. Rule of law in its conceptual sense and how it can be maintained in a real country context is a good place to start.

Margaret Thatcher, Prime Minister of Great Britain had this to say about 'rule of law'.

> "Our abiding commitment to the rule of law is the very bedrock of our civilization. It is what makes all else possible, from the flowering of the arts to the steady advance of the sciences. The idea that men must govern themselves not by the arbitrary commands of a ruler but by their own considered judgment is the means whereby chaos is replaced by order. Balanced by the peaceful resolution of differences, the rule of law and the institutions of representative democracy are what stand between civilization and barbarism. It is through law-governed liberty that mankind has been able to achieve so much"
>
> (Margaret Thatcher, AM OUTLOOK, 2000)

1.1. Rule of Law: A Foundation for Resource Governance in Central Africa

A good place to start in this contextual analysis of the potential usefulness of *Rapprochement* as a framework for growing useful policies and effective institution in Central Africa is this notion of 'rule of law'. The notion of 'rule of law' is central to natural resources law enforcement, governance and trade, therefore crucial in analyzing resource policies and the institutions responsible for their implementation. It can also help improve understanding about the sometimes, selective preference for the supremacy of State power over more participatory processes in resource governance. Analyzing rule of law vis-à-vis the notion of *Rapprochement* can help mediate traditional belligerents of natural resources; State authorities on the one hand, and ordinary folks in day-to-day interactions with natural resources, on the other. Finally, using examples of some resource conflicts drawn from the region can provide a good illustration of how these notions plays out in real life in Central Africa.

1.1.1. Rule of Law and Opportunities for Rapprochement

To understand how the notion of rule of law can relate to *Rapprochement*, 'rule of law' should be perceived in three related perspectives;

Firstly, according to Dicey, (1982) rule of law is "the absolute supremacy or predominance of regular law (a nation's guidelines for governance) as opposed to the influence of arbitrary power, or even discretionary authority on the part of a constituted government[1]". The emphasis in Dicey's thesis is on 'law content' or the substantive quality of policy guidelines as a way of shaping public behavior.

Secondly, F. A. Hayek (1994) makes the argument that, 'rule of law' refers to when a government in all its actions is bound by rules fixed and announced beforehand -- rules which make it possible to foresee with fairness and certainty how the authorities will use their coercive powers in given circumstances, and to plan the affairs of individuals or groups on the basis of available information and the choices that the information suggests. Hayek's thesis requires that, confidence exists between authorities and ordinary citizens regarding how collaboration is to be perceived and valued, or benefits shared and rights protected. There is also an indication of *process* and expression of '*fairness*'. Both characteristics are used by Hayek to qualify the notion of 'rule of law'. This suggests that policies under a context of 'rule of law' should

[1] Government here refers equally to central, local or regional governments authority structures

possess a service value as a process, not just an instructive one, and serving a just, societal purpose.

Thirdly, according to Shen (2000) 'rule of law' refers to formal or procedural justice. To Shen, this denotes "the method of achieving fairness in decision-making; by consistently applying rules and procedures that shape the institutional order of the system". Formal or procedural justice according to Shen, consists of a number of principles; first, the system of laws must have a complete set of decisions and procedural rules that are fair; second, the fair rules of decision and procedure must also be pre-fixed, pre-announced and seen to be done transparently and consistently. Here, Shen also brings in the essential element of process, of deliberation and dialogue, in evaluating the effectiveness of a context of 'rule of law' under which policies operate. Note in this latter analyses by Shen (2000) that, 'rule of law' is also concerned with process and procedure as it is with substance or content. Over three decades earlier, Selznick (1969) had also argued that, "legitimacy" in policies has to do mainly with how the rules are made and applied rather than with their contents. Therefore, in a combined way, what needs balancing in these analyses and applications of 'rule of law', are both ensuring substantive value (content) and fairness as described by Dicey (1982); as well as respect for process and procedure (Shen, 2000).

So, without fair procedures, there are few guarantees that the resulting policy guidelines will be fair; or that, substantive justice will be attained through the institutions created to implement them. In summary therefore, procedures applied transparently and fairly as part of a process are necessary conditions for achieving substantive and just outcomes in natural resources governance under a context of 'rule of law'.

Unfortunately, with overall governance being weak and representative democracy in its infancy, only expedient parts of these crucial notions of 'rule of law' are applied in many central African States.

Two practical cases with which to illustrate this notion are ongoing processes of decentralization in two important Central African States – the Democratic Republic of Congo (DRC) and Cameroon. It can be hypothesized that, in both countries the full spectrum of 'rule of law' must be grasped and applied if decentralization in control of common resources is to produce the needed transformations. Huge potentials exist within existing legal texts in both countries, bold policy adaptations and processes, applying the full spectrum of 'rule of law' to bring together national actors and test progressive policies in innovative ways, to benefit the very poor, need to be taken.

The specific cases of the DRC and of Cameroon presented below, illustrate two situations which can be re-characterized under ‘rule of law’. They also provide different opportunities for *Rapprochement*; one related to the simple existence of regular law (DRC) to support Reducing Emissions from Deforestation and forest Degradation (REDD+) and the other, perceptions of the governance of regular law (Cameroon) as it is interwoven with legality or illegality in forest resources access.

i) The legal context of Readiness for REDD+ in the Democratic Republic of Congo as opportunity for *Rapprochement*

In the DRC, readiness for Reducing Emissions from Deforestation and forest Degradation (REDD+) appears to present excellent opportunities for *Rapprochement*. In this context, *Rapprochement* as framework for a new relationship between the central State and ordinary citizens is supported by the 2011 Constitution of the DRC.

Firstly, this Constitution of 18 February, 2011, laying down law No. 11/11 of 13 July 2011 of the DRC, provides guidelines for administering and sharing of benefits from common resources. This policy lays down the guiding principles for resource control powers between the central State, the provincial authorities and the collectivities. In article 171 of the constitution of the DRC, the texts uphold the distinctions in spheres of influence between the central State in Kinshasa and that of the provinces and collectivities.

Secondly, Article 171 is further supported by the decentralization law No. 08/016 of 07 October 2008. This related provision to Article 171 of the 2011 constitution, further separates jurisdiction over common revenues and resources between the central State, the provinces and collectivities. These provisions therefore establish legal basis for equity in eventual sharing of benefits for a possible REDD+ Scheme.

Decentralized services such as provincial and other territorial jurisdictions in the DRC work to ensure proximity of State services to ordinary citizens. Nevertheless, these local centers of administration remain auxiliaries of central State power, and if misapplied can still separate ordinary citizens, even at that local levels from participating in the benefits from common resources.

Decentralization is a democratic instrument which helps ensure that, given limitations in communications and public participation in governance, the responsibility to administer use of common resources can be extended well beyond the central State, into the periphery of administration. Potentially therefore, decentralization can significantly facilitate the notion of *Rapprochement* bringing actors working together. Nevertheless, unless the intended spirit of decentralization (as an instrument of devolution and democratic governance) is correctly understood and applied in the DRC, physical separation between the central State and provincial authorities might still not produce intended outcomes, even under a context of *Rapprochement.*

Therefore, for the legal situation in the DRC to cement the essential linkage between legality in policies and legitimacy of resource use, an essential element - 'rule of law', must guide that relationship. Rule of Law in the context of *Rapprochement* — would constitute substantive and enforceable elements of procedural rules, iteratively developed through participation of actors, communicated and evaluated transparently by the actors. Under a situation of rule of law, policies will then be evolved which can translate to positive social change for ordinary citizens.

An important question is however, how the legal context for readiness for REDD+ in the DRC is linked to the intuition of Rule of law.

To begin establishing this linkage, policies and the related actions of institutions should be viewed, not as prescriptions or instructions resulting from a precise scientific or administrative decision-making process. Instead, policies and the actions of institutions should be viewed as experiments and therefore, must constantly evolve by evaluating trade-offs and alternative courses of action in the light of new information and competing demands by the powerful and by the less powerful. For instance, whether policies and actions of institutions are perceived as having succeeded or failed should necessitate continuous feedback and corrective measures. Such iterative perception of policy and institutions is only possible if all actors can take credit for successes, or blame, for setbacks. In this context of shared responsibility, a real-time implementation framework of *Rapprochement* or 'coming-together' of the administrators and the administered may become more relevant.

Furthermore, the substantive elements of policies – such as specific regulations and guidelines, must aim continuously to shape public behavior not just of the less powerful, but of all citizens. Therefore, 'rule of law' under an experimental policy and institutional context should intuitively be perceived within a defined timeframe and to operate at multiple sectors and levels. Within this timeframe, defined aspects of substantive policy choices; regulations and guidelines, are to be evaluated in terms of how they produce desired behavior patterns amongst actors. A central feature of this timeframe is therefore, the conduct of the deliberations under the defined context of 'rule of law'. The DRC is beginning this process, so theorizing is possible and exciting. However, Cameroon has been down this road for over a decade. For this reason, the Cameroon example can provide useful lessons for the DRC.

ii) Perceptions of governance under existing decentralization of forest policy as opportunity for *Rapprochement* in Cameroon

Where laws exist and have been tested for some time, interpreting rule of law in the context of *Rapprochement* can significantly help reconcile conflicting perceptions of legality and of legitimacy in natural resources use. One case with which to illustrate the potential for *Rapprochement* in reconciling notions of legality and of legitimacy is the assessment on ‘illegal logging’ in Cameroon (Cerutti and Tacconi 2008, Lawson and McFaul 2010) as this plays out under the 1994 Forest and Wildlife laws, perceived at the time of enactment as a model for forest policy decentralization. Such an appraisal can also help stimulate important discussions about uniting ‘perceptions’ and ‘reality’ in natural resources governance in Central Africa; even in redefining relationships between actors. Uniting intuitions and reality to evaluate social change in real terms is therefore, another important rational and basis for *Rapprochement.*

One version of the report on illegal logging of forests in Cameroon carried a cover photo of a sawn-timber market in Yaoundé, Cameroon, with the accompanying sub-text:

> “The trade in illegally harvested timber provides a living for more than 45,000people,
> a major source of income for corrupt officials and not a cent for the State”
> (Pye-Smith, 2010)

According to this narrative by Charles Pye-Smith (2010) the legitimacy of livelihoods strategies of 45,000 families is qualified as rooted in ‘illegality’ and facilitated ostensibly by ‘corrupt government officials’. Suppose that, the 45,000 people are household heads. If we assume a conservative figure of five persons per family [45,000 x 5], we have 225,000 [a quarter of a million] people living off the proceeds of supposedly illegal activities in order to provide legitimate life-supporting services to their families. Note the ‘*no cent for the State*’ insinuating loss of legitimate [and statutory] earnings by the one party that enjoys absolute supremacy in matters of legality (Dicey, 1982). Obviously, the 225,000 persons would be benefitting from proceeds of illegally acquired goods, despite the apparent legitimacy of household heads providing education, healthcare, housing, feeding and payment of bills for their Cameroonian families!

It is important to note however that, the likelihood of the photographed timber having been harvested outside the law is not been challenged. However, something [reality or perception] has to be out of place, in 'real' terms when one stands back to observe that 225,000 Cameroonians [a quarter of a million] enjoying services that should make the State happy, and in fact save the State considerable resources – have to do so outside of the law.

That, according to the report, those charged with enforcing the substantive elements of State law, appear to have stronger incentives to obtain *rent* from actors as they work to transfer direct benefits to their families - a quarter of a million Cameroonians, and themselves, operating outside the law.

All-in-all, it seems like both the citizens [subjects of the law], and the State officials [upholders of the statutes] choose to operate outside of the law. So who does the law actually serve? Is it possible that, the entire conception of this type of 'rule of law' is actually at the root of the problem? Does it have to do with the way these laws have come about? Have been enacted; i.e., the procedures, the transparency, the participation, or the lack of it? Are there opportunities or lessons learned from this process that could be used in a new context of growing useful laws and effective institutions?

Note that, in order for the so-called 'corrupt officials' to obtain rent from traders or middlemen/women who are in the process of transferring real benefits to a quarter of a million Cameroonians they must physically come into contact with these 'actors'. Firstly, we observe however, in this 'encounter', a *corruption* of *Rapprochement* [coming together, but doing so for the wrong reasons] to break the law. Secondly, we observed that 'State officials' as referred-to in the report have an incentive to privatize what is supposed to be 'public property' so they can derive private rent from it. Between the State officials, the timber agents and their families, there is no one left – only the broken laws! Is it possible that an opportunity to redefine the relationship – one of *Rapprochement* between the State, State officials, traders or middlemen/women and forest dependent communities is being missed?

It is obvious in many of such reports on Central Africa that, many pundits lean heavily on Dicey's (1982) argument of 'rule of law', especially how it emphasizes the absolute supremacy or predominance of regular State law. Relatively less emphases is placed on Hayek's (1994) and Shen's (2000), arguments, for procedure, deliberation, dialogue and to analyze forestry law enforcement in terms of its accountability to ordinary citizens and the needs of their families.

Unless a *Rapprochement* brings together actors by design and is instituted and applied at multiple levels to achieve dialogue, transparency and evaluation of effectiveness of policy, such as in the forest sector, the benefits of decentralization in contexts like the DRC and Cameroon will be delayed.

Finally, if the case of Cameroon with long-term experiences in forest law enforcement governance is highlighted it is easy to see that governance challenges are especially difficult to resolve through traditional means. This is due to behavior patterns and interests that have become entrenched. Most of these behavior patterns and interests have historical, socio-economic and geopolitical roots which cannot be easily unraveled through scientific analyses and policy recommendations alone.

Although *Rapprochement* is proposed in this book, its success will ultimately require taking a step back and looking at Central Africa from a broader global perspective; and to appraise what form *Rapprochemen*t should take at regional, national and local levels in order to be effective.

1.2. Inspirations for *Rapprochement* from Global Experiences

Over many centuries, European countries have cultivated deep interest in Central Africa's natural resources. These interests have become entrenched and now contribute significantly towards shaping the priorities of the Central African Governments that took-over from the colonial administrations over five decades ago. Today, Central Africa's natural resources are sought-after by multinationals not just from these former 'colonial masters', but from other rapidly developing and emerging economies, mainly from Asia. These old and new relationships have strongly influenced recent dialogues on policy and on 'reforms' of institutions in much of Central Africa. Thus, since gaining independence, central African countries have used important opportunities for developing policies and institutions mainly to strengthen export markets of raw materials as well as attract Direct Foreign Investments (DFI).

It is therefore not uncommon to find existing natural resources policies and related institutions appearing to provide greater support to foreign multinationals or to their surrogates, than they do in support of critical economic activity by national level entrepreneurs or ordinary citizens, let alone by grassroots communities or low-income urban dwellers. Such outward orientation of natural resource politics by Central African countries especially regarding raw material exports from the region, contrasts somewhat with the vision of policy development by some of the world's leading societies and economies.

In the United States of America in particular, policy analyses as we know it today was popularized in post World War II military planning by Think Tanks; noteworthy of which, is the RAND Corporation (http://www.rand.org/about/history.html). Since then, policy analysis in the United States has drawn on concepts from different disciplines: economics, political science, sociology, public administration and history; to emerge as a sub-discipline in the 1960s. Similarly, policy analysis also has its intellectual roots in political analysis and in the development of the economic concepts of cost benefit analysis in the 1950s.

Well funded in the late 1960s, by Lyndon B Johnson's Great Society, policy analysis was extended from the national security realm, to other essential services; or to '*bread and butter'* or basic livelihoods issues. Like in much of post-WWII Europe and East Asia, the priority areas of Lyndon B Johnson's Great American society included; infrastructure, portable water, human and animal health, education, poverty reduction and food security – American citizen's issues or grassroots issues. Like in much of Central Africa today, these focus on citizen's issues or on "bread and butter" issues were supported by the State Constitutions of the United States and even of States of post WWII Europe and East Asia.

We also observe in Central Africa that, natural resources (e.g., forest resources) are directly associated with the livelihoods of some of the poorest and most deprived communities in the region – even in the world. As a result, many rural and low-income urban populations, where poverty is strong, depend directly and indirectly on forest products and services of all kinds. Despite this, and unlike in LB Johnson's USA or Post WWII Europe and East Asia, major, policy instruments in Central Africa countries dealing with the forestry sector in particular are not explicitly defined and pursued to support '*bread and butter'* needs of these national groups whose economic survival appears to be directly linked to forests. If anything, the economic interests of these populations are designed to be addressed, through indirect, re-distributive mechanisms, based on taxation, national budgets and public investments – often too complicated to directly stimulate local entrepreneurial practices.

As a result, it is very common to find the relationship between the wellbeing of ordinary citizens and forest products [a source of export revenue for the State], being defined on the basis of legality or of illegality. In fact, numerous regulatory texts around tree products essentially separate the 'State' from the ‘citizens’ in the matter of natural resources use. Substantial numbers of policies and mechanisms exist today that specifically prohibit, thereby separating ordinary citizens from direct use of different forest resources. As mentioned earlier if this separation, with historical, geopolitical and socio-economic roots is to be bridged, entrenched interests and differences would have to be bridged. As we observed with the ‘illegal logging’ appraisal of Cameroon, some of these differences and interests are linked to conflicts of perception over legality and of legitimacy of resource use, ownership and control. But as we observed with situation of regular law in the DRC opportunities exist for bridging some of these conflicts of perceptions and of interests.

Finally, these perceived separations or lack of continuous entente between those charged with making public policy decisions and ordinary citizens in Central Africa has historical and geopolitical roots. Understanding how these may have influenced the status quo of positioning by Central African states vis-à-vis their collaborative relationships with external partners, can help design a more effective framework for *Rapprochement,* grow useful policies and new, effective institutions.

1.3. Possible Conflicts of Interest and Implications for *Rapprochement*

Like in North America, Europe and East Asia, States in Central Africa came into existence under Constitutions that generally proclaimed to support the rights of their citizens. Despite this, because Central African States have remained weak relative to their external economic and financial partners, ordinary citizens continue to struggle economically and socially; often not enjoying critical rights, especially to natural resources. Part of the reason for this is that, the policies of Central African Governments and the institutions charged with their enforcement still remain too responsive and sensitive to signals coming directly or indirectly from international commercial interests, often at the expense of grassroots interests. There is room for co-existence.

Similar signals also originate from multinational companies that lobby international financial institutions; from foreign investments arms of rapidly growing economies, or from their surrogates. Policies and institutions developed at national level under the influence of such multi-lateral and or bi-lateral entities, have thus, generally served to facilitate Direct Foreign Investments (DFI), Foreign Aid or export markets for raw materials from central Africa. These relationships remain useful to economic growth and resource governance. However, in re-thinking how to grow even more useful policies and institutions that are more responsive to local needs, there is need now to concede that predominantly serving the interest of DFI and FDA can sometimes have detrimental impacts on local interests, even if these may have been unintended. Therefore, policies driven to support some international instruments [especially in the area of market competiveness or international trade] should equally be recognized as having the potential to conflict with national and local level economic and social objectives in the same sectors.

With growing commodities scarcity in international markets driving pressures to secure cheap land; and continuing socio-economic difficulties in central African countries, DFI or FDA practices sometimes come into conflict with local livelihoods that depend on the land. On the decision making side, conflicts between FDA and local livelihoods will occur due to separation between administrative decision-making processes and everyday priority setting by rural populations and low-income urban dwellers. Such separation can drive and deepen conflicts of perception between grassroots interests and that of their representatives on the one hand; and between community interests and the agendas of DFI and FDA as presented by the State, on the other. Under such circumstances, a situation of divergence can exist between the priorities of ordinary citizens and the actions of the Government. This can also further complicate the current applications and perceptions of the practice of 'rule of law' on the ground, where it tends to uphold the interest of sitting State authorities, while conflicting with the interests of ordinary citizens.

In such a situation of separation, the biggest losers are almost always the most vulnerable groups. It is thus logical to assume that, a strategy of *Rapprochement* may provide an equitable solution.

Without *Rapprochement* or coming together of the parties, the current scenario which picks winners and losers amongst citizens will continue to persist. In managing forest resources [above or below ground] on which numerous communities depend, who wins or who loses, between the vulnerable and the influential at national level shouldn't be a choice Central African societies are forced to make when committing to a policy option. *Rapprochement* can ensure that, desired outcomes of economic growth and social development become the central driving forces for policy development.

Without *Rapprochement*, fear of losing control by one party will always be the basis for policy choices. Under *Rapprochement*, policy choices in resources management are likely to be driven by positive intent by the actors for the greatest good. Some contexts, in which ineffective policies operate today in Central Africa, can be characterized by fear expressed by some powerful State officials of losing their positions; or struggles between competing commercial interests; often leading to public policy decisions that create new constraints and complexities. Under a context of *Rapprochement*, such constraints can be avoided or lessened. For instance, wide incidence of bureaucracies and corruption can come about as a result of failing to deal transparently and fairly with constraints and complexities involved in forest resources management, such as with the incidence of 'illegal logging'; perceived differently by different groups. As a result of this, some very expensive mechanisms, including satellite tracking of logs from source to eventual market have been proposed as solutions. Such solutions, often beyond the reach of national governments often create complexities and constraints so that, they rarely constitute real measures of progress in development performance. This is so because 'solving problems' in the forestry sector in Central Africa, rather than 'making progress through application of solutions is very so often the goal of many policy processes where the critical actors remain effectively separated. Secondly, complex solutions fail on the first principle of innovation – the cost may outweigh the real benefits.

On paper, good natural resources management policy texts exist in most Central African States. Implementation of these texts however demonstrates that, the concept of rule of law is yet to be fully grasped and consolidated as important actors continue to remain separated from each other and often hold conflicting perceptions regarding what is legitimate; and therefore how policies [legality] should serve social development.

The influence of external development partners in the natural resources policy sector continues to remain overwhelming. As some of these influences have historical roots in the colonial era, they can also be a source of conflicts between what is statutory and what is legitimate to livelihoods at national levels. Either way, the influence of DFI and FDA prerogatives can often eclipse the focus of policies and institutions on the social and economic development priorities of communities who depend on these natural resources for their livelihoods. A strong potential however, exists for *Rapprochement* to help blur disparities in perceptions between powerful and less powerful actors and even help blend-in, the interests of external development partners.

Finally, the historical, geopolitical and socio-economic context of Central Africa presents challenges that must be internalized as a part of *Rapprochement*. There is however, a need to ensure that, the knowledge required to enrich policies and guide institutions actually make it to the intended beneficiaries. Unfortunately, this transition from knowledge to action as a part of policy and institutional development has for many decades in Central Africa been more of a slogan than a reality.

In Chapter II that follows, some analyses is provided to both improve understanding of the challenges faced in the transitions from knowledge to action and why a framework of *Rapprochement* may provide some answers.

Chapter 2

Knowledge to Action through Policy in Central Africa

2. Policy Change in the Context of Constraints in Knowledge to Action

2.1. Why a Re-Think of Policy Analyses in Essential in Central Africa

Physical science teaches us that; *Work* is said to be done, when the point of application of a *Force* moves over a *Distance*; say from point A to point B. If we consider progress with human development to be Work (*W*), then *W* will only come about when the combined effect of the *Force*, denoting economic activity, policy and social action can happen faster and more robustly than any disruptive, or resisting functions (such as *Resistance, Friction*) working to slow down or stop growth, development and positive changes in behavior.

Such driving forces or *Work* leading to human and institutional development in Central Africa depends on a combination of known and unknowns; often complex, notional, social, economic, ecological and political processes working together in complex ways (constituting *Resistance, Friction* or potentially *Accelerators*). Intuitively therefore, the nature of policies and institutions (a part of the *Force*) needed to produce the desired *Work* effect (development) must generate a combined forward *Momentum* (transformational and effective) greater than the slowing down or stopping effect of *Resistance, Friction* or obstructions opposing that forward movement.

But if these combined; policy, political, scientific and technical, organizational, market, geopolitical, social and economic variables remain difficult to unravel in real-time; or their expected positive synergies ineffectively harnessed and applied to the problems, there is very little chance that solutions can be produced on which to apply innovation. Such complexity can even be comparable to the analogy of the ancient Greek Mythology of 'the Gordian Knot'. Only an approach based on near real-time responses, possible only when actors are constantly working together in a *Rapprochement* can cut through such overwhelming complexity, over which no single person or institution can have control. Where actors; those charged with making public policy decisions for natural resources management, and those whose access to those resources we desire [as a matter of equity] are deliberately brought together and monitored as a single team, capacity and consensus for greater effectiveness and innovation, is more feasible in near real-time. When addressing poverty and natural resources governance, without *Rapprochement* or shared responsibility, problems may appear intractable as they do in Central Africa. One effective way forward could therefore, be by changing the environment of the solution through a new cooperative arrangement. Here is how:

There is strong inter-relatedness in human-ecological systems today (e.g., land use, poverty and climate change). When these combine with dynamics in human interests and decision-making the situation becomes even more complex. Under such complexity the capacity for innovation and solutions for transformational action can easily be exceeded. To mitigate such risk, positive change must therefore seek to eliminate or reduce the complexity. One way to reduce complexity is by shortening the process from problem diagnosis through solution design and knowledge generation to action. *Rapprochement* or bringing together the actors can shorten this process by changing the context of the solution. Strong *Rapprochement* between those making decisions; those generating information to inform the decisions, and those whose livelihood depend on those decisions, can help reduce complexity and provide quick responses. Only processes that can engender near real-time responses may be effective in achieving such results. The status quo of physical and temporal separation between problems diagnosis and analyses; knowledge generation, policy formulation, action and assessment of impact, can no longer produce effective solutions under today's complexity in human-ecological systems. Another option with potential to produce similar results is use of high technology. But this requires training and investment infrastructure and therefore more time.

Human settlement centers in Central Africa are expanding; there is rapid outmigration of high quality human resources, rural poverty is becoming endemic, whereas fossil-fuel based economies remain very exposed to global economic shocks. As forest resources degrade and biodiversity erodes in the face of significant and complex changes in land use, there is need for game-changing, even radical re-think of how to evolve effective policies, useful institutions, and how these use information (not just data) to meet these challenges on a continuing bases.

This latter question of how information is used is illustrative of the status quo of policy and institutions analyses in Central Africa.

Currently, three broad types of policy and institutions analyses can be described for Central Africa. These comprise; (i) structural or macro-economic analyses dealing with global and international relationships; (ii) administrative and policy process analyses, dealing with national issues of policy-making, functioning or the lack thereof, of the policies and institutions; and (iii) change-oriented analyses, often dealing with grassroots, citizen rights or the lack thereof [can operate at international as well as at national level].

Structural and macro economic analyses have helped produce bilateral and multi-lateral conventions and agreements (e.g., Voluntary Partnership Agreements, Forest Law Enforcement Governance and Trade Agreements, Climate conventions, etc). Administrative and policy process analyses have helped produce recommendations that are used by donors and other bi-lateral and multilateral partners (e.g., the 1994 Forest and Wildlife Laws of Cameroon and associated application texts, the Forestry Code of 2002 in the DRC, numerous Policy process analyses and publications). Recommendations from administrative and policy analyses are often dutifully presented and or handed to Governments and Ministry officials. Results of change-oriented analyses (e.g., conventions on indigenous people's rights, conventions on women's rights, conventions for prior informed consent on access to natural resources by indigenous peoples, etc) are also used by donors, bilateral and multilateral partners, often through indirect channels. All these efforts can constitute *Force* in the physical science analogy. Despite these, unfortunately, little *Work* can be said to be done (due largely a lack of movement and a sense of common direction). One reason for this (especially at national level) is that, some of the conventions benefitting grassroots communities many have been publicly embraced but privately ignored (*obstructions and friction*) by influential stakeholders whose interests are threatened by them. So at best, despite the huge effort made (*Force*), under conditions of continued separation of the parties (lack of *Rapprochement*), only very moderate goals (actual

Work) are being met. A lack of *Rapprochement* can also make policy and institutional actions reactive or arbitrary, thereby further sapping their potential for transformation.

All three types of policy analyses in Central Africa can be said to be reactive; by this is meant, the analyses preceding their coming into force are performed either to facilitate a program pushed by a donor, on an investor, by a bi-lateral or multilateral actor, or one entirely commissioned by them. The second; policy process, administrative analyses and activist reports on the other hand, can be performed by knowledge centers, individual analysts/consultants or other nongovernmental organizations. Often following a call, itself based on a pre-conceived diagnosis. These often produce scientific publications, reports, policy briefs, etc, that are sparingly used by Government officials, if at all. Despite the usefulness of these second types of policy and institutions analyses, the processes and their products are often one-off activities performed by stakeholders of natural resources management whose livelihoods may not be directly affected by resource management problems.

Furthermore, of these three most commonly used types of analyses, only the policy process and third type; activist analyses would require substantial incorporation of critical historical accounts, grassroots socio-economic processes and organic political development processes in their interpretation. Very often, whether such activist analyses are accepted as mainstream and adopted in policy processes is determined by the extent to which these contextual aspects of history, culture; equity or lack thereof are incorporated in their recommendations. But even where such broad-spectrum analyses have been performed evidence is not strong of substantial integrative efforts exploring how these dimensions of history, politics and socio-economics have combined to produce unique behavioral pertains that are significantly impacting natural resources management (or mismanagement) in Central Africa. One reason for this is that, such essential complexity is more common in analyses of grassroots issues. It is here that all the disciplines meet in a complex mélange of resource-poor livelihoods, power play and competing interests. And traditionally, priorities at this level of analyses rarely make it to the highest levels of national and international decision making. When they do, they are either at the bottom of list, or would require additional funding for their implementation.

Overall therefore, due to such lack of strongly linked analyses between actors; their history and problems (in the absence of conscious *Rapprochement*), assumptions have been made of knowledge-to-action pathways through policy, which have proven to be tedious, expensive, yet ineffective for rapid, substantial and lasting positive change in natural resource management in the region.

Drawing from these insights, it can be argued that methodological and contextual lapses in past and current policy and institutions analyses may have contributed towards producing systemic weaknesses in the knowledge to action trajectory through policy in Central Africa. Finally, building on from the physical science analogy, here is how *Rapprochement* for long lasting, positive social and economic change can be attained;

The hazards of obstruction and frictions inherent in the knowledge to action pathways can be minimized. This so, by bringing actors with authority and power to catalyze solutions, together with those requiring the empowerment of that authority and power, for economic activity in a near real-time scenario. By doing this new complexities will be created. However, these new complexities under a context of *Rapprochement* will be complexities of the *solution*; and not of the *problem*. It is to this type of complexity that innovation can be effectively applied leading to desired growth and transformation.

More advanced economies in Europe, the Americas and Asia are showing that, progress comes with applying innovations to productive human effort or by building on success, and not by incessantly dwelling on problems that have proven intractable. Therefore, the idea of *Rapprochement,* seeks, not to solve problems through use of intermediary products of analyses or of international conventions [that have shown their limit], but by creating opportunities for solutions, using near real-time information in a context of continuing *Rapprochement,* and to which innovations can be applied.

As we contemplate how *Rapprochement* – or directly bringing actors together, may work for Central Africa, we must beforehand, confront what constitutes this *Resistance, Friction* or obstructionist *Forces* in the policy, institutions and knowledge environment in Central Africa.

2.2. Constraints in the Transition from Knowledge to Action

Like many new concepts introduced into Central Africa, policy analysis methods (Dye 2007, Loomis and Helfand 2001, Nagel, 1999) have both built-in, empirical considerations and notions of logical thinking. During formal policy analyses, empiricism and logic can both, be often condensed in the merits of 'the scientific method'. Less considered in numerous analyses however, are critical aspects of context and complexity. As a result, it can be hypothesized that, conceptual and practical conflicts between science and policy-making using knowledge; enterprise and social development; corporate identity, image and reputation, versus engagement for impact; have all conspired to render transitions from knowledge to action, when mediated by policies and institutions, problematic.

For instance, in numerous cases in Central Africa, the traditional goal of policy analyses has often remained one of generating '*savoir-faire*' or knowledge, for scientific articles, reports, formal written recommendations, policy briefs, directives and or technical guidelines. However, a problem here has been that, determinations of *savoir-faire* products are largely shaped by the entities themselves who are generating the knowledge (or limited by their tools); by those funding the work, or by those providing national level legitimacy for the results. Despite the best intentions, actors whose livelihoods are expected to be transformed by the application of that *savoir-faire* are not often significantly involved in diagnosis, design and implementation.

In some unclear way these *savoir-faire* products are intended for those charged with making public policies and other decisions. And the assumptions [rarely evaluated] are that these decision-making 'targeted groups' will 'consume' these well-written materials, change their behavior and make the required public policy decisions. These decisions [sometimes based on sound published science] will then positively impact grassroots communities [who hardly participated in the process]. This is a common, ongoing, but dangerous misconception at many levels.

Note: a common saying in Central Africa goes that, "*the best way to hide knowledge from regional stakeholders is to put it in a publication*!" So unfortunately, while these products may be widely read outside of the region, they rarely get consumed by the intended target audiences, in the intended ways. This reality is not new. In fact, anecdotes about how publications are neither read nor widely used to make public policy decisions are common in Central Africa.

Despite this awareness and set-backs to past and present knowledge to action pathways, why is it radical re-thinks of policy change and institutional reform remain uncommon in Central Africa? Could the answer lie in the logic of another physical process - Newton's first law, where motion in a straight line continues until *an unbalanced force* acts on that body in motion?

In our context of unrelenting, less-than-effective, policy analyses and development, what could constitute such *unbalanced force*? Is it logical that, such *unbalanced force* (i.e., a tendency, not in-balance or in-tune with current beliefs or mindsets) may come in the form of a challenge to the current ethos and or a challenge to the complacencies? Can instituting new and unorthodox approaches to achieve behavior change; i.e., challenging the current uneasy balance between the centre and peripheries of power in natural resource control, become the *un-balanced force*? Is this then a possible case of two negatives delivering a positive outcome? Where the enemy of my enemy becomes my friend?

To buttress these intuitions, I make three observations below, about current transitions from knowledge to action, through policy change and reform of institutions. For purposes of consistency with the analogy of Newton's first law of motion, I will caption these observations, *forces in balance with the current hampered trajectory of policy change and reform of institutions*. Note that 'in balance' here refers to maintenance of the status quo of ineffectiveness in policy change and reform of institutions. By inference, *Rapprochement* as a concept - or bringing actors together, then becomes the antithesis of these 'forces in balance with', or 'in tune with' maintaining the ineffective status quo – it may well become the '*unbalanced force*.

Further, I break up these intuitions into non structural, structural and combined structural and non structural forces in balance with the status quo. Structural forces in balance with the status quo simply denotes - *resulting from current institutional or Government structure*. Meanwhile, non structural forces in balance with the status quo refer to the behaviors by *individual scientist or of institutions* carrying out the policy analyses. I leave it to the reader to make further deductions or inferences from these different intuitions and in doing so reach their own conclusions.

As individual analysts, scientists and nonprofit institutions prepare themselves for impact, using various innovations, they must contend with traditional and nontraditional constraints; some structural and others non structural, with potential to diminish the impact of their initiatives. Below I deal with some structural and non structural constraints to the transition from knowledge to action, perhaps observed in Central Africa, but never before described in this way.

2.2.1. Structural Constraints

2.2.1.1. Administrative Consolidation (AC): The Phenomenon

From a policy and institutions stand point, a climate resilient, central Africa society will be one in which the priority of the vulnerable land user is synchronized with the 'evolving decision-making authority' of the more powerful. However, some contexts present impediments to such transforming engagement, even when there is broad agreement in favor of significant change. One such impediment in Central African States is 'Administrative Consolidation'. Administrative Consolidation is the first phenomenon considered to be *in balance* with the current hampered trajectory of policy change and reform of institutions.

Against a need for *Rapprochement*, and in the resource management context of Central Africa, a phenomenon of 'Administrative Consolidation' or AC can be said to exist. In way of simple definition, AC is an 'evolving and disruptive process of decision-making power'. For instance, it is the manifestly troublesome power of AC which ensures that, efforts at policy change and reform of institutions always generate economic growth and development outcomes vastly inferior to expectations. AC is an opportunistic decision-making force focused on resource control, highly dependent on ad hoc, instructions, ordinances, directives, regulations, even framework policies; even in contradiction to the fundamental purpose of State Constitutions. It is AC which frustrates long term flow of benefits to vulnerable sectors of populations, hampering progressive work by local, national and international civil society actors. Finally, it is AC that stands in the way of improvements in overall democratic governance in natural resources management.

In the dynamics of Constitutional democracy, AC sucks out the 'positive energies' from the more gradual process of State/Nation-building, according to the provisions of the Constitutions. As a general perception, the influence of AC is manifest in decreasing magnitude in the six most forested Congo Basin countries, in the order: Cameroon, Equatorial Guinea, Gabon, Republic of Congo, Democratic Republic of Congo and the Central Africa Republic (CAR).

According to this intuitive ordering, Cameroon would be the most 'Administratively Consolidated' and therefore most challenging as arena for policy change and reform of institutions, while the CAR would be the least (most amenable to change).

However, due to the size and diversity of the DRC, its importance for land use analyses, its unique post-conflict challenges in social, infrastructure and economic aspects [which can create dysfunction]; this country presents good opportunities for transformative policy and reform of institutions. More expansive justifications of the country placements in terms of AC are either beyond the scope of this book or lack empirical basis – so will not be dwelled upon at length.

The notion of AC remains a very real intuition, and one deserving of new hypotheses and more in-depth study. Nevertheless, I dwell further below, on the nature and origins of this phenomenon of AC, optimistic that, this will help strengthen the basis for empirical evaluation of the intuition by interested scholars.

Administrative Consolidation is the dynamic and disquieting result of two processes; (i) an evolving and unenthusiastic adaptation by Central Africa States, of the western style constitutional democracy and economic model, and (ii) a prerogative for political and social stability using proceeds from natural resources export and or other expedient means.

Under prevailing AC processes, sitting Government administrations come under regional and or international pressure and receive signals to put in place directives, conventions or ordinances, which facilitate Direct Foreign Assistance (DFA) - Multi-lateral/Bi-lateral Assistance (M/BA), Direct Foreign Investment (DFI) or simply, participation by that Government in regional and international mechanisms. In almost all cases, there is an immediate need for expedient action by that Government. This urgency then compels the Government to take 'all necessary steps' to facilitate the intent of those signals.

This urgency and the continued pressure for Government action encourage ad hoc administrative decision making processes. As these administrative decision processes are repeated, legitimacy snowballs as confidence and infallibility is accumulated. The main protagonists within the administration begin to crystallize and to consolidate. As this process continues, especially within Ministries in charge of natural resources (mines, forests, etc), a hardening core of civil servants [of the relevant Ministry with some co-opted individuals] gravitate to the centre of the 'consolidation' processes. With support and blessings from regional and international organizations and even multinationals commandeering and funding the process this core of 'instructions receivers' aka 'public decision-makers' rapidly become unaccountable to the Constitutional democratic process; and begin controlling the process, the affairs of the Ministries and the livelihoods that depend on the resources they control.

These administratively consolidated processes are notorious for sending the wrong signals to change-agents (civil society, consultants, project leaders, Government officers not belonging to the 'inner circle', etc), who can be misled by these 'signals of change; imminent policy review or institutional reform'. This can send them into an investment spree of lobbying, conferencing, consultations, etc, even causing them to waste valuable resources, raise expectations and dash hopes of reform of the process.

Consider the genesis period of the 2001 Mining code of the Republic of Cameroon. Signals received by the public pointed to ‘Land Tenure Reform’, meanwhile all-along an administratively consolidated core was aware that, the ‘movements’ around the Land Tenure statutes were solely intended to facilitate allocations of mining concessions to multinationals – already at Cameroon’s doorsteps.

The same can be said about the 1994 Forest and Wildlife Laws of the Republic of Cameroon. This was actually a ‘culmination’ of another program - the Structural Adjustment Program (SAP) of 1988 initiated by the Breton Woods Institute of the World Bank. Note that this SAP included amongst others; laws on freedom of association and on liberalization of political parties, compromise on ‘personnel load-shedding’ by the Ministry of Public Service, as well as reduction of salaries of civil servants, followed by the devaluation of the CFA Franc in 1993 by 100%, etc. Much of the ‘additional’ elements in the package of these ‘reforms’ came as a surprise to the majority of Cameroonians – who still feel the effects, for better or worse today.

The current preparation process for reducing emissions from deforestation and forest degradation (REDD+ readiness) in central Africa is also characterized by similar dynamics in which a hardening core of civil servants and international experts appear to dominate the process in each country. Where there has been more progress on REDD+ readiness e.g. in the DRC, pundits argue that, this is led to a significant extent by expatriates and by international organizations, providing advice to a small core of national civil servants. Where progress has been slow to nonexistent (e.g. in Cameroon, Gabon, Eq. Guinea) AC as described, appears to be at an advanced stage. And where progress can be described as intermediate (Republic of Congo and CAR) we observe a mixture of growing AC and a similar process such as in the DRC.

At regional level, similar processes which have facilitated AC include processes like forest certification (led by institutions like the Forest Stewardship Council), forest law enforcement governance and trade (FLEGT) agreements, voluntary partnership agreements (VPA) and myriads of smaller less prominent agreements in the forestry sector. What all these have in common are;

- They all require solid administrative consolidation, ensuring and believing that the interest of the State is being protected
- They are initiated from outside the countries or region,

- They create less, not more freedoms at local and national levels in terms of access to natural resources,
- They are designed to enhance market competiveness of companies already controlling chains of custody of natural products (and commodities) in global markets
- The strongest of these companies are incorporated in Europe, North America and increasingly in Asia.

These momentous processes always have at their core, consolidated teams of civil servants with broad powers, answerable, not to grassroots voters, but to high level politicians and executives in the administration, supported by international institutions or their surrogates.

An essential feature of AC is that it is never driven by need for grassroots representation or a need to promote the constitutional democratic process. It is driven by a need by a consolidated administrative core, answerable to the executive branch of Government to meet urgent political prerogatives. The consolidated administrative core making public policy decisions, can often work with instructions from as high up as the Prime Minister's office or the Presidency.

AC is by no means static. As follow-up to expedient actions, targeted appointments and re-distribution of political power, that is favorable to the decision process quickly follows. The AC process then works to further strengthen and concentrate administrative power and the influence of relevant departments. Often, strong relationships are established between the international beneficiaries of the public policy decisions and administratively consolidated cores. The teams in the Ministries help preserve and sustain the decision outcomes, rendering them impenetrable to any initiatives for greater democracy; transparency and accountability.

Programs springing from such administratively consolidated decision-making then take root and are implemented without the messiness of transparency, accountability, participation and broad communication. The relevant Government departments can then proceed to co-opt other institutions and actors relevant to implant the agenda. A significant outcome of the growth of AC as a tactic of governance and decision-making is the disincentive it engenders for constitutional democracy in central Africa. And in this way the evolutionary growth and development of the constitutional State becomes seriously challenged.

So, whereas the grassroots actors (i.e., indigenous groups, rural people, women, minorities, the unemployed, or other vulnerable group or their representatives), require constitutional provisions to affirm their humanity, uphold their rights and guarantee their advancement as citizen and co-owners of all natural resources, AC creates a strong head wind on these ideals. As constitutional democratic processes are weakened in central African States these grassroots actors are the main casualties.

For instance, under a context of growing AC the impact and influence of Civil Society Organizations (CSOs), even including legislative arms of Government, such as the Parliament can be significantly weakened as decision-making becomes less accessible to the common citizen. Under advanced situations of AC, the *raison d'être* of other critical components of a democracy; e.g., the Media and the Judiciary, can quickly become instruments furthering the agenda of AC, further alienating grassroots actors and weakening the constitutional democratic State.

Lastly, over the past two decades AC in the Congo Basin has been gradually, but relentlessly rendering innovations in transformative policy analysis futile and traditional approaches to same, costly, yet ineffective. It is partly this neutralizing effect of AC that has rendered investments in bottom-up and other forms of campaigns for policy and institutional change ineffective, and discouraged numerous international missions and governance initiatives out of the central Africa region.

Note that, *Administrative Consolidation* is considered here as a structural constraint to policy change and reform of institutions. The next two constraints; the Knowledge Trap and Mission Creep are presented as non structural.

2.2.2. Non Structural Constraints

Two observations presented as nonstructural forces also considered as being *in balance* with the status quo of current hampered trajectory of policy change and reform of institutions are described below. These are

i. *The knowledge trap*; which can create complacency amongst scientists and policy analysts
ii. *The fear of mission creep*: which can terrify innovative organizations away from engaging to build on success for greater impact

The *knowledge trap* and the *fear of mission creep* can seriously hamper the impact of programs. Effective strategies for policy change and reform of institutions should therefore create conditions which discourage these phenomena. However, understanding them better is a necessary first step.

2.2.2.1. The Knowledge Trap

Producing scientific knowledge also happens to be an important goal of organizations and individuals seeking credibility and leadership in policy analysis and reform of institutions. However, when the requirement for publications becomes a centre-piece of an institution or project's existence, it can slow-down or, even impede robust transition of scientific knowledge to transformative action.

Where focus on publications is an overarching priority, drawing-in the non scientific community can also become difficult to achieve or less of an operational priority. Institutions can then become insular, and overly focused on generating knowledge, failing to re-adjust their strategies to include non knowledge goals. When this happens such an institution can be said to exist in a 'Knowledge Trap'.

Where this is the case, a symptom would be that, scientific publications quickly become legitimate end-products, even the sole *raison d'être* of a research and analyses process; including analyses of policy and of institutions. To date, publications [including by many individuals and institutions in the Congo Basin] serve as an achievement by which analysts and researchers are acknowledged by their peers – hence the notion '*to publish or perish'*. Such a notion in my opinion is far too luxurious for a society seeking to build basic institutions for economic development, especially with the history and geopolitical disadvantages enjoyed by Central Africa States.

Unfortunately, in the absence of substantial knowledge to action mechanisms, a legitimate knowledge focus by scientists can quickly become incentive even for policy analysts and project managers to follow-suit and remain complacent. The knowledge euphoria can lull 'victims' into becoming less hungry to seek progress at a different or higher level of change such as engagement with those charged with making public policy decisions at multiple levels where transformation can happen.

Awareness of the dangers of the knowledge trap alone is hardly sufficient for change because of its positive correlation with another constraint - the fear of mission creep.

2.2.2.2. Mission Creep

How often do we hear colleagues saying 'we shouldn't be doing this, or that?' That, the mission or mandate of our organization does not allow us to go that far! Or, that action constitutes mission creep, and is beyond the scope of our institution's mandate? These are scenarios commonly encountered in challenging resource management settings; the more complex the milieu, the more likely the scenario.

Venturing outside one's mission is generally considered undesirable because of the danger that, each success breeds more ambitious attempts, often stopping when a final, sometimes, catastrophic failure occurs. The expression, 'mission creep' first appeared in articles concerning United Nations Peace keeping missions during the SOMALI War (Washington Post, April 15, 1993 and New York Times, October 10 1993). Mission creep is of particular importance, as it has consequences for impact and can be reinforced by the project management cycle.

(i) Fear of mission creep can impede impact

Like policy analysis itself, the notion of 'mission creep' has its roots in military science. In its most common applications 'mission creep' refers to the expansion of a project or mission, beyond its original goals, often following initial or unexpected successes. Rigid work plans, donor funding cycles and or budgets that may not be stretched, often set limits on an organization's portfolio of activities.

The fear of mission creep, describes a situation where an organization has to constantly balance how much it needs to be in its comfort zone as an entity and how much exposure it can tolerate to achieve impact.

Being 'comfortable' as an institution and 'achieving impact' should not be mutually exclusive. However, achieving impact in unfamiliar, problem contexts sometimes require testing the mission boundaries. Unless balance is achieved between the boundaries of an organization's mission, and staying in its comfort zone, policy research for change, can become isolated from real-world decision making that transforms. This isolation can be created by a fear of mission creep.

Under fear of mission creep, any chance of moving on to influence policy adaptation or reform of institutions, beyond laid-down outputs, can then be viewed legitimately as beyond the mandate of a project.

(ii) Project implementation and mission creep

With growing appeal of some 'private sector' project management methods, nonprofit institutions are themselves (very mistakenly in my view) adopting a wide range of private sector practices (while conveniently excluding the essential element of 'risk-taking'). Two of these are the 'restricted funding' and 'the project cycle management' notions. As a trained Resource Manager myself, I will argue that, these and other corporate notions coming out of business schools; have weakened, not strengthened the mission-focus of nonprofit organizations.

At best, the 'restricted funds' and 'project cycle management' notions are largely corporate prerogatives. They help organizations stay within bureaucratic guidelines. Depending on how these are understood and applied, these management approaches can nevertheless reinforce the fear of mission creep. Policy and institutions analyses should therefore, take these into consideration also, if such policies and institutions are to significantly change the operating environments of projects.

(iii) Project cycle management and mission creep.

The 'restricted funding model' and 'project cycle management' notions can today also have impacts on missions of organizations. These models are now exerting increasing influence over nonprofit organizations, and placing limitations on organizations' missions. In some cases these bureaucratic notions have been sub-consciously re-interpreted as basis for a conservative or even 'restrictive management agenda' for projects.

In today's complex world of integrated natural resources management these project management tools can impact how projects perceive and achieve lateral and vertical synergies, eventually, impact. Whereas management decision-making within organizations is often one-dimensional (discretely targeting single or multiple issues at a time) impacts in the field are almost, always synergistic, multi-dimensional, multi-level and sometimes unpredictable.

However, Managers and drivers of single-dimensional corporate decisions remain aware of the possibility that, their actions through their organizations may be multi-dimensional, even unpredictable. It is partly this awareness which can create a fear factor of 'unintended consequences of decisions' to pursue or not to pursue a 'risky' line of action, even if there is possibility for big impact. It is often at this point of pre-emption of unintended consequences; that those charged with making decisions in nonprofits organizations exhibit the highest sense of the 'fear of mission creep'.

Finally, there is good awareness by nonprofits operating on the nexus of human development and environmental conservation that, problems and their likely solutions remain complex. Therefore, isolating and achieving desired impacts and outcomes from these complex contexts remain very challenging. How then can organizations achieve impact under such conditions of complexity, where challenges occur at multiple scales and at multiple levels?

If mission creep is inevitable, yet abhorred, how then can positive energy for impact be generated at that point of greatest fear or of opportunity?

(iv) Positioning for impact in a context of fear of mission creep

Some organizations have traditionally established balance between achieving impact and managing mission creep by periodic re-branding, or through internal and external performance evaluations. During such events, there can be revitalization of project staff. However, depending on evaluation formats used, participating partners, clients and beneficiaries can benefit from realignment with the essence of the organization's mission, goals and values. Evaluation of relationships between project staff and external stakeholders can help narrow the divide between an organization's missions, its partners and beneficiaries, and help achieve impact even in a context of fear of mission creep.

Despite this potential for impact by bringing actors together in real-time [or *Rapprochement*]; existing internal evaluation tools used by organizations for appraising the value of networking as a part of overall performance remains rudimentary. Instead, internal evaluation instruments in many organizations remain focused on appraising and rewarding insular, internal relationships based on internal responsibility metrics. Insufficient attention is thus paid to relationships with external partners, even when these may be closely tied to the organization's mission and envisaged impact. In today's rapidly changing problems contexts, such as in Central Africa, systematic insensitivity by an organization to its external environment may spell danger. By maintaining close and dynamic relationship with its external context, an organization can keep its values, yet remain sensitive to its mission and goals as these evolve in the problem context. Paying attention to these external relationships should therefore be a part of internal recognition and rewards mechanisms as a motivational and actualization tool.

Fear of mission creep remains legitimate, however for inward-looking organizations, insensitive to the external environment, the boundary between where mission creep ends and impact begins, may be fuzzy. The inability to appraise for external relationships during internal performance evaluations can encourage and consolidate inward-looking posturing and threaten impact. Such posturing can tend also to be strongest in organizations most afraid of reputational risks, of mission creep, even at the expense of impact.

Isolation and inability to evaluate external relationships thus enhances fear of mission creep. Therefore only closer, multi-scale, multi-sector and multi-level engagement by a project, with the problem context, can provide satisfactory change outcomes. Furthermore, only strategies that allow close and constant iteration and visualization of the big picture of the problem context can realistically minimize the pitfalls of mission creep. It is such clarity that can enable managers to minimize risk.

Similarly, critical outcomes and impacts in complex policy and institutions contexts, attained through synergy can be perceived to be just beyond the mandate of the project. Partnerships, networks, sub-contracting, out-sourcing, etc, are all scaling out, approaches used by nonprofits to reach goals without direct engagement themselves. These relationships continue to flourish, although some of the assumptions underlying them may be questionable. Whether alone, or in partnership, achieving impacts may require nonprofits to look beyond their comfort zones and to internalize the risks of mission creep through multi-level, multi-scale engagements with a problems-solutions context. All these can be facilitated by a comprehensive grasp of the notion of *Rapprochement.*

Below, I present a third obstacle, the Science - Policy gap, as a combined nonstructural and structural constraint to effective policy change, reform of institutions and transition from knowledge to action.

According to this better known concept, the Science - Policy divide can separate knowledge from becoming action; can re-enforce both the Knowledge Trap and Administrative Consolidation, and can even deepen the fear of Mission Creep by organizations.

2.2.3. Combined Structural and Non Structural Constraint

2.2.3.1. The Policy - Science Divide

The policy – science gap is a broadly understood concept in the domain of public policy development using knowledge and information generated by empirical. Some notable works in this domain have been carried out by Bradshaw and Borchers (2000), Lemons (1996) and Manning (1988). Of specific relevance to this present discourse, is Manning (1988), where he articulated a conceptual separation between the different ways science and policy handle elements of 'uncertainty' inherent to all scientific information; in scientific hypothesis-testing and policy decision-making, respectively. According to this work (Manning, 1988), the basic rules by which policy and science operate governs the manner in which both disciplines handle uncertainty in the transition from knowledge to action.

This analysis by Manning points to a complex transition from knowledge to policy action, separated in a significant way by the radically different ways in which science and policy treat uncertainty. According to that intuition, whereas science handles uncertainty as an essential part of all information; to be acknowledged, even measured, and communicated openly; policy considers uncertainty as a weakness to be concealed, or even a reason to discard entire bodies of information. It is within this divide that institutions generating knowledge can become locked in a *knowledge trap* fearing the perils of uncertainty and masking this as fear of *mission creep*, especially if required to develop engagement strategies for impact.

In a similar way Government administration can become 'consolidated' in complacency by isolating themselves from uncertain information. Governments then become vulnerable to ambitious multi-nationals or other aggressive direct foreign investors, in whom they find certainty, receiving signals, around which they consolidate very quickly.

As an illustration of the transition from scientific knowledge to policy actions and institutional reform, consider the analogy of a chemical reaction from; 'reagents' transitioning to 'products'.

Suppose in Figure 1 below where, relevant scientific knowledge is denoted as 'reagents, A'. This combines with 'reagents, B**'**, denoting administrative decision-making, to produce C, D and or E, F. Thus A + B in timeframe T1 then transitions into another timeframe T2 to achieve C and D (or expected, complementary outcomes), or E and F (or unexpected, uncomplimentary outcomes), at different levels and timeframes.

According to this intuition (Figure 1), failure to bring knowledge systems and decision-making power together correctly, and in a timely manner, can lead to the triple jeopardy of

i. Administrative consolidation,
ii. A knowledge trap and
iii. Increased fear of mission creep

However, a desirable condition may exist where uncertainty about different types of information is internalized through '*Rapprochement*' between knowledgeable actors (reagents A) and those charged with making public policy decisions (reagents B) engaged for policy change and institutional reform.

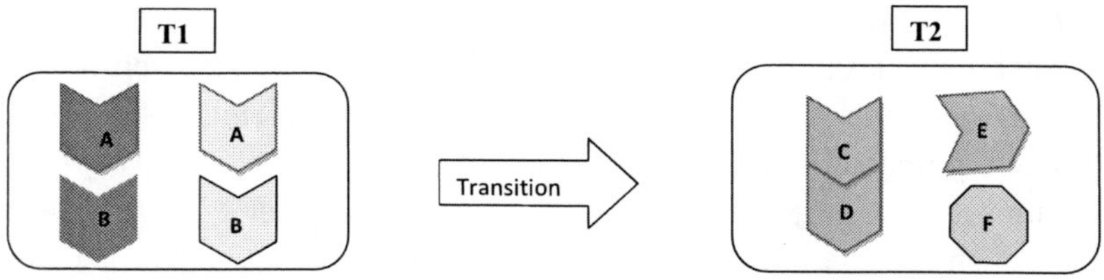

Source: Developed for the Rapprochement concept.

Figure 1. Transition from science to policy with and without '*Rapprochement*'.

Under another scenario, behavior change, new practices and new products (C, D) can be produced at T2. This new, desirable scenario is the essence of *Rapprochement* envisaged in this process.

Where there is no '*Rapprochement*' (or coming together) there is likelihood of new, but deformed outcomes (denoted as E and F) at time T2. This is likely to be caused by prolonged administrative consolidation (by those charged with making decisions in public institutions), or from complacency by knowledge centers locked in a knowledge trap; or lack of real-time engagement with the problem context, caused by their fear of mission creep. These deformed, unintended outcomes can keep stakeholders apart and in disharmony, rather than coming together and risking solutions and promoting innovation. Entities fearing risk will always have difficulties innovating.

The more persistent the separation, the deeper the disharmony, so too does administrative consolidation strengthen. The knowledge trap can deepen as institutions find more justifications (such as fear of mission creep) and complacently re-define themselves as just 'knowledge centers of excellence', performing actions, 'moving the goal post of impact' and remain in their comfort zones. These positions held by stakeholders can become even further entrenched, moving them further and further apart and eventually changing their form – making *Rapprochement* at a later date, impossible (e.g., E and F at T2 in Figure 1). This may happen even while actors may seem to exist in the same 'collaborative', physical space.

The science and policy divide is however, not as abstract as the intuition here may suggest. In fact, in the Congo Basin in general, tremendous efforts are being made to bring scientific knowledge, policies and institutions together. These are manifested in the numerous environmental and forest management platforms; such as the Conference on Dense Humid Forest Ecosystems in Central Africa (CEFDHAC), the Congo Basin Forest Partnership (CBFP), Governance Working Groups (GWG), and many others.

Platforms like these, typify the goals of creating direct and indirect channels of communications through which grassroots organizations, research and State institutions can interact at local, national and regional levels to influence Government policy and functioning of institutions.

A number of examples of constructive engagements or of *Rapprochement* in which such associations, platforms and mechanisms are 'instrumentalized' to help in forest resources management governance can be described for the Congo Basin. I mention here, the Governance and Biodiversity Working Groups in the Congo Basin (many exist in the region), and the German Technical Cooperation (GIZ) through its facility the Pro – PSFE or Forest and Environment Sector Program (ProPSFE). Like these working groups (e.g., IIED's Governance Working Group, Convention on Biological Diversity Working Group, etc) the ProPSFE's approach is one of very close and direct '*Rapprochement*' between actors such as the Ministry of Forest and the Environment at national levels and COMIFAC (Central Africa Regional Commission on Forests) at regional level.

Another format of collaboration for policy influence is that of the "Discussion Circle of Partners of the Ministry of Forest and Wildlife (MINFOF, Cameroon) or CCPM. This is a group of international and national nongovernmental organizations, sitting on an ad-hoc basis with officials of the Forestry Administration. Both strategies (ad hoc CCPM and or semi-permanent Pro-PSFE) for '*Rapprochement*' seek to bring knowledge closer to decision-making to influence policies and reform institutions.

From a theoretical perspective, Bradshaw and Borchers (2000), helps us to understand the transition from one extreme of separation between knowledge and those charged with making public policy decisions; to another of '*Rapprochement*', ownership and action. They describe how an intermediate period of resistance to new information can be described as a period of *cognitive dissonance* (or period of resistance to information). Bradshaw and Borchers (2000) further articulate how, such resistance to information and the knowledge it embodies, can gradually and eventually become one of acceptance and ownership as actors come together physically and intuitively. They characterize this new situation as one of *volition* (or of willing acceptance) in the case of this present proposition - of '*Rapprochement*'. Therefore, willful acceptance of information, despite uncertainty can occur as decision-making priorities become more closely aligned with the nature of problems and needs of society. Under this scenario of '*Rapprochement*' between knowledge centers and Government administration, there is a lower likelihood of the triple jeopardy of 'administrative consolidation, a knowledge trap and increased fear of mission creep.

Therefore, *Rapprochement* or 'coming together' to produce action, from knowledge, during the volition or acceptance phase will be effective, only if it addresses a number of basic questions; (not necessarily an exhaustive list)

1. What specific knowledge is available and what remains uncertain or unknown?
2. Is the available knowledge what is needed at that specific moment in time?
3. Can the uncertainty or its impact be quantified?
4. To what extent does the uncertainty if incorporated in that knowledge, increase the risk that a catastrophic mistake will occur?
5. If the uncertainty cannot be avoided, can the actors sufficiently and robustly identify and manage it?
6. What is the risk that the uncertainty poses for *Rapprochement* between the actors coming together?

Without such bases for *Rapprochement*, awareness and timeliness in responses to threats caused by uncertainty may become impossible. In a similar light, effectiveness in policy change and reform of institutions will require that, certain opportunities are not missed and certain actions if not taken at the right moment, may not produce the required benefits. So we can ask the following additional question;

- How then should *Rapprochement* between knowledge centers, beneficiaries, clients of programs and those charged with making public policy decisions be organized before, during and after the volition or acceptance phase?

Despite the best efforts at *Rapprochement*, cognitive dissonance or deep-seated resistance to different viewpoints on information can still persist, and 'administrative consolidation' and the 'knowledge trap' may become inevitable. Due to these likelihoods, both phenomena (administrative consolidation and the knowledge trap) should not always be viewed as threats to be avoided. Being self-preservation mechanisms themselves, both can be rolled back to uncover important change processes and possibilities for innovations. For this reason it should be stated that 'administrative consolidation' and the 'knowledge trap' should only be truly considered constraints, when they prevent a transition from knowledge to action in which,

- The benefits of knowledge to action are very clear to actors
- These benefits and the beneficiaries have been prior identified
- The likely behavioral change given the context represents the intended project/process outcomes.

Rapprochement is about opening up opportunities for sustainable management of natural resources, reducing poverty and promoting economic growth. Adapting policies so that they are useful to people and in reforming institutions to efficiently execute their responsibilities should consider the following;

- Clear knowledge of the problems being addressed
- Knowledge of what solutions have been applied to the problems and how these have faired
- What strategies to adopt to ensure that actors with decision-making power are accessible to victims affected by the problems at these levels;
    - Across different production sectors at the micro - local and administrative level
    - Across different production sectors at the meso - administrative and political process level
    - Across different production sectors at the macro-economic and higher administrative level

The greatest impediments to a vision to unravel constraints like 'administrative consolidation' and the 'knowledge trap' are context specific issues. These are often impossible to address without critical immersion in the context of the problem. Such an immersion will ultimately facilitate a determination of how knowledge will be shared during engagements in a context of *Rapprochement*, between different types of actors at different sectors of production, levels and scales of decision making.

2.2.4. Final Words

These final words will re-visit the main structural and non structural constraints possibly complicating attainment of significant social and economic impact through policy and institutional analyses in Central Africa. These final words will reflect the main purpose of this book, this counsel - to serve as basis for action on *Rapprochement*; by governmental and nongovernmental entities. Donors and nongovernmental entities can benefit from introspection about whether passive, traditional approaches of analyses, publications and recommendations can still be relied on to deliver expected outcomes – in the hope that States will, on their own take the needed actions.

To the willing reader, this book should not be viewed as a traditional publication; presenting results of analyses and deductions. Instead, it should be appreciated as an experience-based handbook on decision-based development and change, to guide actions that seek policy and institutional reform. Such relevant works seeking to evolve and grow good policies and effective institutions to support natural resources management in Central Africa should preferably be actions in progress. Although there are numerous ongoing works in the region which can benefit from this counsel, the author prefers not to mention each project by name but preferring to let readers to objectively consider the propositions and to adopt or reject them as they see fit.

The Central Africa context is complex and very young, and therefore the rules and procedures that will emerge from application of this counsel and be validated or not by actors, will themselves be experiments whose outcomes will be monitored closely and evaluated on an ongoing basis.

For the western educated and intellectually versatile (probably most people who will read this document), it is easy to expect results in a Central African context along the lines of expectations for Europe, the Americas and Asia when making analyses. From a methodological standpoint the deep differences between Central Africa and more developed societies, are not often explicitly admitted when selecting tools, making analyses and interpreting results. As a result of insufficient contextualization [even using similar methods], many donors, international institutions and professionals working in the field of natural resource policies in Central Africa do not see Central Africa clearly enough in terms of its context; history, culture, socio-economics and mixtures of these.

Consequently, many conclusions can actually lead to more bottlenecks being created, than solutions, produced. It is in this likelihood of ineffective hypotheses and methodological approaches to policy and institutions analysis in Central Africa, that the notion of *Rapprochement* as framework for policy and institutional impact can perhaps finds it's rational.

For all the natural and human resources promise, Central African States, sixty years after independence are still basically, loose collections of people and communities, pulled in many directions by the ambivalence of traditions, ethnicity; struggling to maintain unclear relationships with former colonial countries, while balancing those loyalties with new, forceful foreign investors. Added to these relationships, these countries continue to reluctantly accommodate overwhelming democratization pressures from powerful bi-lateral and multi-lateral entities. In the face of these pressures, Central African nations, being full members of the United Nations and numerous other international forums, are compelled to think of themselves as sovereign States, and therefore to assume the stature and responsibilities that come with full-fledged nationhood. Sitting side by side with nations, cultures and civilizations like the United States of America, France, China, United Kingdom, India, Brazil, Russia, and Arab nations can cause Central African nations to act in some ways like them – believing in themselves as being a full part of an international community of nations.

The reality is can be very different and such honesty must be the basis for urgent introspection in Central Africa. Central Africa faced enormous challenges making its own decisions before the rise of sophisticated economic forces like China, India or the European Union hungry for Central Africa's natural resources. These pressures are more intense today and unless Central Africa can craft ways to maximize participation by its millions of citizens in economic development affairs, Africa may not adapt and compete well in this transformed international market place. Without applying the full force of benefits from its natural resources, Central Africa cannot build the infrastructure and human capacity required to fully adapt to social and environmental changes that have come to this region. Without mobilizing the full potential of her human resources in the international space and in the Diaspora, Central Africa will remain completely unaware of what needs to be done, such as what is, and has happened in more advanced economies – knowledge that she requires for its own survival, and needed to become competitive.

The divided model of governance in which a small group of Government officials, with dominion over all natural resources, working to develop the country for the populations is producing painfully slow results, certain to be overtaken by threats facing Central Africa. The fruits of a democracy dominated by unfamiliar concepts of multiple parties and by prerogatives of elections without equal emphasis on rule of law, protection and growth of private property, are failing to engender productive collaboration between citizens. Like much of Africa, Central African citizens through a mixture of poorly managed external and internal relationships are in a State of perpetual conflicts of interest with each other.

Due to these complexities; some historical, others induced by contemporary events, it is impossible for success to be achieved through some simple, rational scientific process, where results are then applied to problems, by a seating authority, for the benefit of all. The only viable course of action is by compelling citizens to work together, cultivate and grow new rules and procedures for enforcement and review by them. Central Africa must be supported to involve as many of her citizens as possible in governance and these citizens within and without the regions, must take full responsibility for the region's successes as well as for her failures. *Rapprochement* is a framework for governance with potential to make that happen.

Now, a few words on the main structural and non structural constraints discussed in this book. Firstly, Administrative Consolidation – the phenomenon stifling transformation in Central Africa, is a direct result of Central Africa's relationship with powerful forces in the international community. These include international organizations, bi-lateral and multilateral donor organizations. This phenomenon cannot be unraveled by the citizens of Central African countries alone. Support must come from the international community. An effective first form of support from the international community should be to use the intuitions in this book and others like it, as hypotheses, and to test these hypotheses by identifying, characterizing this phenomenon of Administrative Consolidation and to engage these States at the highest level with specific proposals to open-up decision-making processes to greater participation through effective decentralization. Re-directing traditional support to significantly include civil society organizations is one effective mechanism to strengthen decentralization and citizen participation.

Secondly, international institutions must become more aware of their fear of mission creep and the extent to which through their own actions, they may be in a knowledge trap. Advanced economies in the Americas, Europe and Asia did not get to where they are today by not changing from within. To get to this new normal, the USA went through a war of independence, even a civil war, a bill of rights and decades of economic growth and rule of law. Europe went through two wars, numerous structural reforms and re-construction, including the post-WWII Marshall Plan and today the European Union. Japan,

South Korea and other Asian mega economies also went through similar transformations and massive support from powerful western economies. India, Indonesia and Brazil benefitted significantly from agrarian and technological revolutions. These required periods of introspection, even mild forms of isolationism. China, the World's second biggest economy went through all these transformation and is still basically a Maoist, command economy. Managed liberalization in China has produced perhaps the most transformative economy the world is yet to see. Despite enormous foreign assistance, Africa in general and Central Africa in particular is not at its 'normal'. For Central Africans themselves and their partners to treat Central Africa as if it has reached its 'normal', like some of these older, more accomplished or accomplishing economies is a mistake. FDI and FDA have not produced transformation in central Africa partly due to lack of internal and endogenous restructuring. For instance, it is urgent for institutions working in Central Africa to evolve strategies for action which are transformative in outcome, pro-active in their orientation to results they seek but deliberative and democratic in operational style. Central Africa will not achieve positive transformation at the speed necessary to roll back retrogressive forces to achieve growth if it simply applies principles from more advanced economies as if it has reached its 'normal' – it has not. Without rule of law, high technology and large, educated private sector, Central Africa will not be transformed by 'western' medicine – where everyone is just doing her/his work efficiently.

Such growth may happen in European, North American, and some Asian economies that may have reached their optimum or 'normal'. Central Africa has not – not even close, and requires significant restructuration. Fear of mission creep by reputed and capable international organizations preferring to remain in their comfort zones, and risking knowledge trap in the process may represent a missed opportunity for Central Africa. Central Africa needs what the best institutions in the world have to offer. More than ever, the core values and missions of some of the best institutions and organizations in the world are critical to transformation in central Africa. The complexity of central Africa must not be a reason for these institutions and donors to disengage. Such disengagement only impacts negatively on the millions of citizens in the region who are separated from decision-making and therefore who lose the most if separated from the core values and missions of these international organizations that helped built stronger economies and nations. It is important that such leading institutions find ways to engage, re-brand or re-structure if necessary, remaining true to their missions but accepting adaptable methods in given central African contexts – geared at achieving positive, lasting outcomes.

Finally, Central Africa must deal urgently with its ambivalence – one foot in irrational aspects of customs and traditions and one foot in modernity and the logic of science. Nevertheless, science is having a significant impact on Central Africa – such as mobile technology. But this is not driving growth – it is simply driving consumption of goods and services. Science in central Africa must become relevant to the everyday lives of millions of citizens who lack education, training, skills and earning power to lift themselves from poverty. National and international centers of knowledge working in Africa should help make science relevant to ordinary citizens. Achieving this requires that all scientific research activities within Central African countries need to either build human capacity in specific ways, such as building empirical analyses skills. Science in the region should also produce products and practices which deliver solutions in key livelihood areas of food production, food storage and distribution; nutritional security, portable water, affordable energy, sanitation, habitat improving, valuing biodiversity and ways to take care of the environment which does not require repressive actions. A framework for *Rapprochement* bringing citizens, scientists and Government together around the table on a continuous basis can reduce misunderstandings, internalize scientific uncertainty and help quicken the transition from scientific hypotheses to changing lives. One effective way to bridge this science –policy-action gap and begin building an indigenous transformation consciousness based on a new partnership between science and politics is by promoting adaptable frameworks of *Rapprochement* at local, meso and national levels.

LIST OF TERMS

The following terms have been explained in the context in which they have been used in this book.

Accelerators: Factors which can enhance rapid social and economic development

Access rights: The freedom to enjoy full benefits from forest resources without being perccived as breaking the law.

Accountability: A condition in which the actions of public officials is sensitive to the priorities of citizens and recognizes citizens issues as the raison d'être of their employment.

Activist: A more direct (as opposed to passive) approach to addressing a development problem via policy. One based more on already established, known rationale and justifications.

Actors: Those directly involved in the process of policy development, likely to be directly affected negatively and positively by failure or success, respectively.

Actualization: Describes management processes in organizations that enhance a sense of fulfillment in the personnel

Administrative consolidation: Describes the incidence within State administration of a hard core of decision-makers, receiving instructions from higher up Government hierarchy and especially insensitive to calls for greater transparency and participation

Aka: Also known as

Analysts: Natural resources management policy professionals working independently or within national and international organizations

Anecdotes: Popularly held beliefs in the region, not necessarily scientifically proven

Authorities: Civil servants representing the views of the Central State but operating at local, regional and national levels.

Belligerents: State authorities on the one hand, and ordinary folks on the other, in day-to-day interactions with natural [forest] resources.

Beneficiaries: Actors who stand to gain from good policies and effective institutions inside and outside the country.

Bi-lateral: One-on-one political, cultural, scientific and trade relationships between foreign countries and Cameroon or the Democratic Republic of Congo.

Biodiversity: All forms of life existing in Central Africa's forests and other ecosystems.

Bread and Butter: Everyday issues of wellbeing of ordinary citizens; food, portable water, energy, habitat, basic infrastructure, etc.

Broad spectrum: Expert analyses of policy and institutions that encompass historical, contextual, scientific, social and economic questions.

CFA: Currency of the Central African Financial Community [Currency of Central African States]

Chains of custody: The system of forest products certification, such as by the Forest Stewardship Council that helps customers choose forest products from sources that contribute to global conservation, community based and other forms of sustainable forest management.

Climate change: Warming of the atmosphere due to the accumulation of so-called green house gas emissions from deforestation and forest degradation

Codification: The process of developing legal codes from policy procedures, statements of intent, etc.

Cognitive dissonance: The discomfort, even resistance when an actor simultaneously holds two or more conflicting viewpoints ideas, beliefs or values.

Collectivities: Communities of local people organized to serve as auxiliaries to centralized or decentralized administrative authorities

Colonial: During colonial times when Central African countries were under direct rule by European countries

Comfort zone: The position taken, often by international organizations working in Central Africa, to not engage too closely with institutions.

Commodities: These are goods, either raw or semi-finished products, exported from Central African countries and traded on global markets; and include coffee, cocoa, solid, liquid minerals, rubber, oil palm, etc.

Common resources:
Refers to forest resources, such as would occur in unclassified forests whose legal tenure is not held by any one actor; or community held forest products not subject to a strict management plan

Communities: A collection of people living in and around forests and depending on it for their livelihoods.

Conferencing: Organizing conferences in response to impending reforms of natural resources management processes.

Conflicts of interest:
Differences in perceptions between government administrations and ordinary citizens in terms of access, ownership, use and management of forest resources

Consolidation: As applied to Administrative Consolidation, refers to a tightening inner circle of decision makers holding to their viewpoint and not open to critique

Conventions: A formal, written agreement between parties

Correlation: A dependent relationship between two processes or variables, where existence of one necessarily impacts on the other.

Corruption: Actions and processes that go against acceptable practices – or 'going against the grain'.

Decentralized and centralized:
Refers to State services with national responsibilities (centralized) and those located outside administrative capitals with local responsibilities

Deliberative: An iterative process of participation

Devaluation: An official reduction of the exchange rate of the CFA Franc

Diaspora: African experts living and working abroad but retaining interests and skills needed to collaborate with institutions working in the forestry sector within the sub-region.

Foreign Direct Investment (FDI):
Direct investment into production or business in Central African countries by companies in foreign countries, either by buying a company in the local country or by expanding operations of an existing business in that country

Directive: A legislative Act of the Government

Distance: Distance is a numerical description of how far apart objects are. Here, *Distance* refers to the separation between decision-makers and ordinary citizens; between development goals set and attained.

Empirical: A source of knowledge acquired by means of observations and or experimentation

Empowerment: Possession of knowledge and awareness that one's action is legitimate, legal, is expected, and is likely to contribute significantly to social and economic progress

Equity: Every mechanism in place to enable different actors involved in forest resources management to have full legal and legitimate access

Force: In physics, a force is any influence that causes an object to undergo a certain change, either concerning its movement, direction, or geometrical construction. In this book *force* represents the sum total of positive intents and actions by institutions and policies to bring about positive social and economic change.

Forest certification: Linked to the notion of Chain of Custody and refers to the process that helps customers choose forest products from sources that contribute to global conservation, community based and other forms of sustainable forest management

Forest Law Enforcement Governance and Trade Agreements (FLEGT):
Refers to a European Union led convention with Central African States which commits them to high standards of

forest governance practices and control of illegal activities in forest management

Fossil-fuel: Fuels formed by natural processes such as anaerobic decomposition of buried dead organisms, e.g. coal, oil and gas, because these have been formed from the organic remains of prehistoric plants and animals.

Framework policies: A logical structure that is established to organize policy documentation into groupings and categories that make it easier for employees to find and understand the contents of various policy documents.

Friction: In physics friction is the force resisting the relative motion of solid surfaces, fluid layers, and material elements sliding against each other. Here it refers to countervailing forces holding back the sum total of intents and actions by institutions and policies to bring about positive social and economic change.

Fuzzy: 'Not distinct'

Game-changing: 'Innovative' and liable to bring about positive transformation

Geo-political: A policy analysis context influenced by a geographic region, e.g. Central Africa, where weak governance and even poverty is endemic.

Gordian knot: A legend of Phrygian Gordium a figure in Greek Mythology and associated with Alexander the Great; used as a metaphor for an intractable problem - disentangling an "impossible" knot or solving problems by "thinking outside the box".

Governance: Decisions that define *expectations* of accountability, transparency, participation; leadership in management of natural resources

Grassroots: Local level communities in constant contact, and interactions with forests and other natural resources

Hypothesis: A proposed explanation for a phenomenon. For a hypothesis to be a scientific hypothesis, the scientific method requires that one can test it.

Illegal logging: The harvest, transportation, purchase or sale of timber in violation of laws.

Immersion	To be fully conversant with, and engaged in the context of the problems to be addressed by policy and institutional reform
Indigenous:	Local communities or individuals who originate from the immediate area and who have lived in that area; at least as long as records exist
Innovation:	The development of new processes or products with solutions that meet new needs, needs not yet articulated; or use of existing practices and products in new ways.
Institutions:	All formal decision-making entities from the local, through regional levels to the national level. These institutions can be within Government, nongovernmental structures, bi-lateral and or multi-lateral organizations
Instrumentalized:	To be 'used as an instrument'
Internalized:	To fully understand, accept and be a part of the intent, approach and expected outcome of a process or concept as may be applicable
Introspection:	To re-examine an individual's or an institution's conscious objectives, *modus operandi*, and overall method of seeking results and impact
Knowledge center:	All national and international centers, institutes and organizations of research
Knowledge trap:	Knowledge centers that increasingly find themselves generating substantial amounts of information but not perceived by observers to be directly engaging with beneficiaries for impac.
Legitimate:	'The right thing to do' not according to statutory laws, but according to what is rational, logical, and even self-evident
Lobbying:	The act of attempting to influence decisions made by officials in the government, or members of regulatory agencies
Logging:	The extraction of timber from forests
Macro-economic:	The performance, structure, behavior and decision-making of an economy at the national and regional level, rather than at the level of local and individual markets
Mission creep:	Going beyond an organization's official mandate as a result of perceived success within a current time-frame.

Momentum In physics *momentum* is the product of the mass and velocity of an object. Here *momentum* refers to a combination of the effectiveness of actions and policy proposals (representing the velocity component of momentum), and their transformational qualities (representing the mass or content aspects of momentum).

Multi-actor: Many actors working together

Multi-lateral: Refers to Government agencies having investment or other relationship with more than one foreign partner, often donor agencies and donor countries

Multi-level: To operate at more than one level; at local, provincial and national level

Multi-scale: The same as multi-level

Multi-sector: Actions which are taken in more than one government sector; forestry, agriculture, small and medium enterprises, etc.

National Annual Work plans: Work plans prepared by government Ministries on an annual basis

Nonstructural: Constraints which are not directly linked to functioning of an organization or a State

Nuts and bolts: Essential elements or critical content of the process

One-dimensional decision: Management decisions that are linked directly to individual outputs that do not factor in the effects of the output or synergies

Ordinances: Laws generally made at lower levels of the Government

Out-sourcing: Contracting out of an internal business process to a third party organization

Pathways: Mechanisms for action and impact

Personnel load shedding: Downsizing, letting workers of the State go

Post-conflict: The period after a civil war or after other armed civil unrest.

Post-independence: After Independence

Private equity: An asset class consisting of equity securities in operating companies that are not publicly traded on a stock exchange

Private sector: In the forestry sector in Central Africa, operating as large forest concessions with licenses to exploit timber from forests of Central Africa

Protocols: Orderly procedures about how to proceed in experimentation

Reagents: Pertain to the analogy in Figure 1, and refers to inputs in scientific knowledge and Administrative decision making

Real terms: Measurable changes in the lives of beneficiaries resulting from economic activities enhanced by policy and institutional action

Real-time: Refers to creating change or precursors for change 'almost simultaneously' with the action being taken to bring about that change

Real-world: Changes occurring in the everyday lives of beneficiaries

Reducing Emissions from Deforestation and Forest Degradation: An incentive mechanism to reduce green house gas (GHG) emissions from tropical forest loss and degradation. It functions by creating financial incentives to encourage developing countries to conserve and manage healthy, natural forests, reducing GHG emissions, enhancing carbon stocks and sequestering GHGs.

Rent: A payment to an actor in the timber products market chain in excess of that which is required by law, or receiving a lesser payment that facilitates avoidance of the normal process

Resistance: In physics, refers to a measure of the degree to which an object opposes an electric current through it. Here *resistance* refers to countervailing forces holding back the sum total of intents and actions by institutions and policies to bring about positive social and economic change.

Restricted funding: Project funds which cannot be used for any other activity but for the purpose agreed to with the donor

Stakeholders: Different from actors and refers to entities interested in or supporting a resource management process, but who are not significantly affected positively or negatively by either success or failure, respectively

Structural: As opposed to 'non structural' constraints; constraints which are directly linked to the functioning of an organization or a State

Structural Adjustment Programme:
Structural adjustments are the policies implemented by the International Monetary Fund (IMF) and the World Bank (the Bretton Woods Institutions) in developing countries. These policy changes are conditions for getting new loans from the International Monetary Fund (IMF) or World Bank, or for obtaining lower interest rates on existing loans.

Surrogates: Entities acting on behalf of other partners, either in investments or in negotiations

The Administration:
State authorities at different levels

Think tanks: International organizations [most developed in the United States of America] that perform research and advocacy on topics such as social policy, political strategy, economics, military, technology, environment, development, climate change and culture

Unbalanced force: Processes of *Rapprochement* which is not in equilibrium with the intuitive separation between State authorities and local communities in the management of forest resources

Uncertainty: Insufficient knowledge – considered as a given when using results of scientific analyses

Volition: The period during which policy decision makers and scientists have come together in a Rapprochement; in a new relationship where perception of uncertainty in information is reduced and scientists realize that they do not have to test all hypotheses before information becomes useable in policy and actions.

Voluntary Partnership Agreements:
Voluntary Partnership Agreements, or VPAs, lie at the core of the European Forest Law Enforcement, Governance and Trade (FLEGT) Action Plan – the EU's response to a call for action at the 2002 World Summit on Sustainable Development in Johannesburg, South Africa. VPAs are meant to act as a practical mechanism

for identifying and excluding illegal timber from the EU market.

Vulnerable groups: This refers to the rural and urban low-income groups, with a predominance of indigenous groups, the uneducated, women, children who generally use and depend on forest products for a significant part of their livelihoods

Work: In physics, *Work* is said to be done when the point of application of a force moves across a distance. Here *Work* refers to the total driving forces required to bring about positive and long lasting policy and institutional change.

REFERENCES

1994 Forest and Wildlife Laws of Cameroon.

A "Straw Objective" on Adaptation for WRI, 2010: Ensuring Development Succeeds in a Changing Climate, DRAFT.

Bradshaw, G. A. and J. G. Borchers, 2000, Uncertainty as information: narrowing the science-policy gap. Conservation Ecology **4** (1): 7. [online] URL: http://www.consecol.org/vol4/iss1/art7/

Bührs Ton, Bartlett, Robert, V., 1993, *Environmental Policy in New Zealand, The Politics of Clean and Green*, Oxford University Press, ISBN 0-19-558284-5.

Cerutti, P. O. and Tacconi, L. (2008), 'Forests, Illegality, and Livelihoods: The Case of Cameroon', *Society and Natural Resources* Vol. 21, No. 9, pp. 845–53.

Dicey, A.V., 1982, Introduction to the Study of the Law of the Constitution, Indianapolis: Liberty Fund F. A.

Dye, Thomas R., 2007, *Understanding Public Policy* (12th ed.), Prentice Hall, ISBN 0-13-936948-1.

Forestry Code of 2002 in the Democratic Republic of Congo.

Hayek, F., 1994, The Road to Serfdom. Chicago: University of Chicago Press.

Lawson S and L McFaul, 2010, Illegal Logging and Related Trade, Indicators of the Global Response, Chatham House, the Royal Institute of International Affairs, ISBN 978 1 86203 235 4.

Lemons, J., 1996, *Scientific uncertainty and environmental problem solving,* Blackwell Science, Cambridge, Massachusetts, USA.

Loomis John, Helfand Gloria, 2001, *Environmental Policy Analysis for Decision Making*, Kluwer Academic, ISBN 0-7923-6500-3.

Margaret Thatcher, *Follow the Leader*, AM. OUTLOOK, Spring 2000, at 23.

Manning, E.W., 1988, Models and the decision maker, pp 3-7 *in* R. Gelinas, D. Bond, and B. Smit, *Perspectives on Land Modeling,* Workshop Proceedings, Polyscience, Montreal, Quebec, Canada.

Mbile P and Van der Meer E, 2010, Administrative analysis of the Forest and Environment Sector Policy, Final report, *45 pp.*

Nagel, Stuart S., ed., 1999, *Policy Analysis Methods*, New Science Publishers.

New York Times, October 10 1993 http://en.wikipedia.org/wiki/Mission_creep (accessed Nov. 16 20120.

Pye-Smith, C. 2010 Cameroon's hidden harvest. CIFOR, Bogor, Indonesia.

Selznick P., 1969, Law, Society and Industrial Justice, New York: Russell Sage Foundation.

Shen Y., 2000, "Conceptions and Receptions of Legality: Understanding the Complexity of the Law Reform in China", In The Limits of the Rule of Law in China, (eds.) Karen G. Turner, James V. Feinerman and R. Kent Guy. Seattle: University of Washington Press.

The RAND Corporation, History and Mission, http://www.rand.org/about/history.html), (accessed Nov. 16 2012).

Washington Post, April 15, http://en.wikipedia.org/wiki/Mission_creep (accessed Nov. 16 2012).

INDEX

A

access, xii, 6, 18, 19, 27, 47, 48
accountability, 9, 27, 49
adaptation(s), xiii, 25, 30
administrators, 7
advancement, 28
advocacy, 52
agencies, 50
agriculture, 50
ambivalence, 40, 43
antithesis, 23
appointments, 27
appropriate technology, xii
Asia, 10, 11, 21, 27, 39, 41
assessment, 8, 18
atmosphere, 46
authorities, 1, 2, 3, 4, 6, 7, 13, 46, 52
authority, 4, 21, 23, 41
avoidance, 52
awareness, 22, 31, 37, 48

B

behavioral change, 38
behaviors, 23
beneficiaries, 14, 27, 32, 37, 38, 50, 51
benefits, ix, xii, 4, 6, 9, 10, 14, 24, 37, 38, 40, 45
biodiversity, 19, 43
blame, 7
bottom-up, 28
Brazil, 40, 42

C

Cameroon, vii, 5, 6, 8, 10, 12, 19, 24, 26, 36, 46, 55, 56
campaigns, 28
carbon, 51
cash, xii
catastrophic failure, 30
certification, 26, 46, 48
challenges, 1, 10, 14, 15, 19, 24, 31, 40
chaos, 3
chemical, 34
Chicago, 55
children, 53
China, 40, 42, 56
citizens, x, xi, 1, 2, 3, 4, 6, 9, 11, 12, 13, 40, 41, 42, 43, 45, 47
civil servants, 25, 26, 27
civil society, 24, 25, 41
civil war, 41, 51
civilization, 3
clarity, 33

clients, xi, 32, 37
climate, 1, 18, 23, 52
climate change, 1, 18, 52
coal, 48
cocoa, 47
coffee, 47
cognitive dissonance, 36, 37
collaboration, 4, 36, 41
colonial countries, 2, 40
colonial era, 14
combined effect, 17
command economy, 42
commercial, 12, 14
communication, 27
community(ies), x, 1, 2, 9, 10, 11, 13, 14, 19, 22, 29, 40, 41, 46, 47, 48, 49, 52
competing interests, 20
complexity, xi, 3, 18, 20, 21, 31, 42
conception, 9
conflict, 13, 24, 51
Congo, 24, 26, 28, 29, 35, 36
consciousness, 43
consensus, 18
conservation, 31, 46, 48
consolidation, xii, 25, 26, 34, 35, 37, 38
Constitution, 6, 55
constitutional democracy, 1, 25, 27
construction, 41, 48
consumption, 43
contextualization, 39
contradiction, 24
convention, 48
Convention on Biological Diversity, 36
cooperative arrangement, 18
corruption, 9, 14
cost, xiii, 11, 14
cost benefit analysis, 11
counsel, vii, 39
creep, 28, 29, 30, 31, 32, 33, 34, 35, 37, 41, 42, 56
culture, 20, 39, 52
customers, 46, 48
cycles, 30

D

danger, 30, 32
data collection, xiii, xiv
decentralization, 5, 6, 8, 10, 41
decision makers, 47, 52
decision-making process, 7, 13, 41
decomposition, 48
deforestation, 26, 46
degradation, 26, 46, 51
democracy, 1, 3, 5, 24, 25, 27, 28, 40
Democratic Republic of Congo (DRC), vii, 5, 6, 24, 46, 55
democratization, 3, 40
depth, 24
despair, xii
devaluation, 26
developing countries, 51, 52
devolution, 7
dialogues, xi, 10
directives, 22, 24, 25
discomfort, 46
dissonance, 46
distribution, 27, 43
divergence, 13
diversity, 24
donor countries, 50
donors, 19, 39, 42
drawing, 29

E

earning power, 43
earnings, 8
East Asia, x, 11, 12
ecological systems, 18
economic activity, 2, 10, 17, 21
economic change, 21, 48, 49, 52
economic development, ix, x, xiii, 14, 29, 40, 45
economic growth, 13, 24, 38, 41
economic progress, 48

economic transformation, x
economics, 11, 20, 39, 52
education, 9, 11, 43
educational experience, vii
electric current, 52
employees, 48
employers, vii
employment, 45
empowerment, 21
energy, 32, 43, 46
enforcement, x, 9, 12, 41
entrepreneurs, 10
environment, 18, 21, 43, 52
environmental change, xi, 1, 40
environmental management, xii
environments, 31
Equatorial Guinea, 24
equilibrium, 52
equity, xii, 2, 6, 18, 20, 51
ethnicity, 40
euphoria, 29
Europe, vii, x, 11, 12, 21, 27, 39, 41
European Union (EU), 40, 41, 48, 53
evidence, x, 20
exchange rate, 47
executive branch, 27
export market, 10, 12
exports, 10
exposure, 30
external environment, 32
external relations, 32
extraction, 50

F

fair procedures, 5
fairness, 4, 5
families, 8, 9
FDA, 13, 14, 42
FDI, 42, 47
fear, 13, 28, 29, 30, 31, 32, 33, 34, 35, 37, 41
fears, xii
financial, 12, 51
financial incentives, 51
fluid, 49
food, 11, 43, 46
food production, 43
food security, 11
force, 20, 22, 23, 24, 40, 48, 49, 52, 53
foreign assistance, 42
foreign investment, xii, 12
forest management, 35, 46, 48
forest resources, ix, 6, 11, 12, 13, 14, 19, 36, 45, 47, 48, 52
France, 40
freedom, 26, 45
friction, 19, 49, 52
fruits, 2, 40
funding, 20, 22, 25, 30, 31, 52
funds, 31, 52

G

Gabon, 24, 26
geo-political, x
GHG, 51
global markets, xii, 27, 47
globalization, 3
goods and services, 43
governance, ix, xii, 3, 4, 5, 6, 8, 10, 13, 18, 24, 26, 27, 28, 36, 40, 41, 48, 49
governments, 4, 14
grassroots, x, xii, 10, 11, 12, 13, 19, 20, 22, 27, 28, 36
Great Britain, 3
growth, 17, 21, 27, 41, 42, 43
guidelines, xiv, 4, 5, 6, 7, 22, 31
guiding principles, 6
Guinea, 26

H

habitat, 43, 46
hazards, 21

health, 11
history, 11, 20, 29, 39, 56
honesty, 40
housing, 9
human, vii, x, 11, 17, 18, 19, 21, 31, 40, 43
human development, vii, 17, 31
human resources, 19, 40
hypothesis, 33, 49

I

ideals, 28
identification, xiii
identity, 22
image, 22
immersion, 38
improvements, 24
incidence, 14, 45
income, xi, 1, 2, 8, 10, 11, 13, 53
independence, xi, 1, 2, 10, 40, 41, 51
Independence, 51
India, 40, 42
indigenous peoples, 19
individuals, 4, 25, 29, 49
Indonesia, 42, 56
ineffectiveness, 23
infancy, 5
inferences, 23
informed consent, 19
infrastructure, 11, 18, 24, 40, 46
institutional change, xiii, 28, 53
institutions, vii, ix, x, xi, xii, xiii, 1, 2, 3, 4, 5, 7, 9, 10, 12, 14, 17, 19, 20, 21, 22, 23, 24, 26, 27, 28, 29, 30, 31, 33, 34, 35, 36, 37, 38, 39, 41, 42, 46, 47, 48, 49, 52
interest rates, 52
international financial institutions, 12
International Monetary Fund (IMF), 52
international relations, 19
international trade, 13
introspection, 39, 40, 42
investment, 18, 25, 47, 50
investments, xii, 28, 52
investors, 34, 40
isolation, xii, 2, 30
isolationism, 42
issues, 11, 19, 20, 31, 38, 45, 46
iteration, 33

J

Japan, 41
jurisdiction, 6

K

Korea, 42

L

law enforcement, ix, 4, 9, 10, 26
laws, 5, 8, 9, 26, 49, 50
lead, 34, 39
leadership, 29, 49
learning, 3
legality, 6, 7, 8, 11, 14
legend, 49
liberalization, 26, 42
liberty, 3
light, 7, 37
loans, 52
lobbying, 25
local government, xii
logging, 8, 12, 14, 49

M

magnitude, 24
majority, 1, 26
management, ix, 13, 14, 18, 20, 24, 30, 31, 36, 38, 39, 45, 47, 48, 49, 52
market economy, xii

marketing, x
masking, 34
mass, 50
materials, xi, 22
matter, 12, 18
medicine, 42
metaphor, 49
migration, x
military, 11, 30, 52
minorities, 27
mission, 28, 29, 30, 31, 32, 33, 34, 35, 37, 41, 42
missions, 28, 30, 31, 32, 42
models, x, 31
modernity, 43
modus operandi, xiii, 50
momentum, 50
multinational companies, 12
multinational firms, xii

N

national security, 11
natural resource management, 21
natural resources, ix, xii, xiii, 1, 4, 5, 8, 10, 11, 12, 14, 18, 19, 20, 24, 25, 27, 28, 31, 38, 39, 40, 47, 49
networking, 32
New Zealand, 55
nonprofit organizations, 31
North America, vii, x, 12, 27, 42

O

obstruction, 21
officials, 8, 9, 14, 19, 20, 36, 40, 50
oil, 48
operations, 48
opportunities, xi, 6, 9, 10, 12, 21, 24, 37, 38
organize, 48
ownership, 1, 12, 36, 47

P

Parliament, 28
pathways, ix, 20, 21, 22
physics, 48, 49, 50, 52, 53
plants, 48
policy, vii, ix, x, xi, xii, xiii, 1, 4, 5, 6, 7, 8, 10, 11, 13, 14, 15, 17, 18, 19, 20, 21, 22, 23, 24, 25, 28, 29, 30, 33, 34, 35, 36, 37, 39, 43, 45, 46, 48, 49, 50, 51, 52, 53, 55
policy choice, 7, 13
policy instruments, 1, 11
policy options, xiii
political parties, 26
political power, 27
politics, 10, 20, 43
portfolio, 30
positive correlation, 1, 29
positive interactions, 3
post-colonial legacy of separation, 3
poverty, ix, xi, 1, 2, 11, 18, 38, 43, 49
poverty reduction, 11
preparation, 26
preservation, 37
principles, 5, 42
private sector, 2, 30, 42
private sectors, 2
problem solving, 55
procedural justice, 5
procedural rule, 5, 7
professionals, 39, 45
project, xi, 2, 25, 29, 30, 31, 32, 33, 38, 39
proliferation, 2
proposition, ix, 36
protection, xi, 41
public administration, 11
public investment, 11
public officials, 45
public policy, xi, xii, 2, 12, 14, 18, 22, 27, 29, 33, 34, 36, 37

R

raw materials, 10, 12
reagents, 34
real terms, 8
reality, 8, 9, 15, 22, 40
recognition, 32
recommendations, xi, xiii, 10, 19, 20, 22, 39
Reducing Emissions from Deforestation and forest Degradation (REDD+), 6
reform(s), i, iii, vii, x, xi, xii, xiii, 10, 22, 23, 24, 25, 26, 28, 29, 30, 33, 34, 36, 37, 39, 47, 49, 56
regulations, 7, 24
regulatory agencies, 50
relevance, 33
rent, 9
replication, xiii
reputation, 22
researchers, 29
resistance, 36, 37, 46
resolution, 3
resource management, 20, 24, 30, 52
resource policies, 4, 39
resources, 1, 4, 5, 6, 8, 9, 10, 13, 14, 18, 25, 40, 45, 46, 47
response, 47, 53
restructuring, 42
revenue, 11
rewards, 32
rights, xii, 1, 4, 12, 19, 28, 41, 45
risk(s), xi, xii, 2, 18, 30, 32, 33, 35, 37
risk-taking, 30
root(s), 9, 10, 11, 12, 14, 27, 30
rubber, 47
rule of law, 3, 4, 5, 6, 7, 8, 9, 13, 14, 41
rules, xiii, 4, 5, 33, 39, 41
rural areas, 1
rural people, x, 27
rural population, 13
rural poverty, 19
Russia, 40

S

SAP, 26
sawn-timber market, 8
scaling, 33
scarcity, 13
school, 31
science, 11, 17, 19, 21, 22, 30, 33, 34, 35, 43, 55
scientific knowledge, 29, 34, 35, 51
scientific method, 21, 49
scientific publications, 20, 29
scope, 24, 29
securities, 51
security, 43
services, 1, 6, 8, 9, 11, 47
shape, 5, 7
shareholders, xii
signals, 12, 25, 34
social change, xiii, 7, 8
social development, x, 13, 14, 22
social policy, 52
social problems, xii
society, 11, 23, 29, 36
sociology, 11
solid surfaces, 49
solution, xii, 13, 18, 21
South Africa, 53
South Korea, 42
specific knowledge, 37
stability, 25
stakeholders, xii, 19, 20, 22, 32, 35
statutes, 9, 26
stock exchange, 51
structural reforms, 41
structure, 23, 42, 48, 50
style, 25, 42
surrogates, 10, 12, 27
survival, 11, 40
Sustainable Development, 53

T

talent, x
target, 22
taxation, 11
teams, 27
technological revolution, 42
technology, xii, 18, 42, 43, 52
tenure, 47
territorial, 6
territory, xiii
testing, 30, 33
threats, 37, 40
time frame, xiii, 50
top-down, ix
trade, 4, 7, 8, 26, 46
trade-off, 7
traditions, 40, 43
training, 18, 43
trajectory, 21, 23, 24, 28
transformation(s), 2, 5, 20, 21, 29, 41, 42, 43
transparency, 9, 10, 27, 45, 49
transportation, 49
trickle down, xii

U

United Kingdom, 40
United Nations, 30, 40
United States(USA), 1, 11, 40, 41, 55
urban, 1, 2, 10, 11, 13, 53
urban population, 11

V

variables, 18, 47
velocity, 50
victims, 29, 38
vision(s), x, xiii, xiv, 11, 38
visualization, 33
voters, 27

W

war, 41
waste, 25
water, 11, 43, 46
weakness, 34
work ethic, 2
workers, 51
working groups, 36
World Bank, 26, 52
World War I, 11